TO LYNDA--
ON THE OCCASION OF
OUR 8TH ANNIVERSARY--
THIS IS MY GIFT TO YOU....
... AND US, WITH THE "R1
PERSON" FOREVER DOESN'T SE
LONG ENOUGH! THANKS FOR BE
MY RIGHT PERSON, IN THE PAST AND A
MANY, MANY HAPPY RETURNS!!

FOREVER,

Billy

MW00628874

Learning
to
Love
Forever

OR

"THE
TRUE
STORY
OF
BILLY
AND
ZOOBIE"

OTHER BOOKS BY ADELAIDE BRY

Inside Psychotherapy

TA Primer

TA Games

TA for Families

A Primer of Behavioral Psychology

The Sexually Aggressive Woman

est: 60 Hours That Transform Your Life

How to Get Angry without Feeling Guilty

Visualization: Directing the Movies of Your Mind

Friendship: How to Have a Friend and Be One

Learning to Love Forever

A 40-DAY PLAN

FOR A LOVE THAT

LASTS

BY Adelaide Bry

WITH LEONARD FELDER

Macmillan Publishing Co., Inc.

NEW YORK

Copyright © 1982 by Adelaide Bry

All rights reserved. No part of this book may be
reproduced or transmitted in any form or by any means,
electronic or mechanical, including photocopying, recording
or by any information storage and retrieval system,
without permission in writing from the Publisher.

Macmillan Publishing Co., Inc.
866 Third Avenue, New York, N.Y. 10022
Collier Macmillan Canada, Inc.

Library of Congress Cataloging in Publication Data
Bry, Adelaide.
Learning to love forever.
1. Interpersonal relations.   2. Social inter-
action.   3. Sex (Psychology)   4. Love.   I. Felder,
Leonard.   II. Title.
HM132.B77   302   81-23596
ISBN 0-02-517960-8   AACR2

10 9 8 7 6 5 4 3 2 1

Designed by Jack Meserole

Printed in the United States of America

Lines from "If You Could Read My Mind":
1969 EARLY MORNING MUSIC, a division of EMP LTD.
All Rights Reserved
Used By Permission of WARNER BROS. MUSIC

Lines from "Love and Affection":
Lyrics and Music by Joan Armatrading
1976 RONDOR MUSIC (LONDON) LTD.
All Rights Administered in the United States
and Canada by IRVING MUSIC, INC. (BMI)
All Rights Reserved—International Copyright Secured

While there are numerous insightful loving men and women who keep contributing to my expanding ability to love, I want to mention a few who are explorers—charting new ways for men and women to love openly and honestly.

First is Werner Erhard whom I honor and cherish and who has contributed immensely to my life; and also Stewart Emery and Sondra Ray who in their trainings and books have made an excellent contribution.

And my personal dedication is to that persistent gnawing essence which I got from my mother; that essence refuses to let me settle, to blind myself for comfort, to accept what is not true, to always reach beyond myself, to be bigger, and more loving as long as I live on this planet.

CONTENTS

INTRODUCTION

I never thought I could act this way
And I've got to say that I just don't get it.

I don't know where we went wrong,
But the feeling's gone and I just can't get it back.

—GORDON LIGHTFOOT
"If You Could Read My Mind"

I don't know you, Gordon Lightfoot, but I'd like to throttle
you. You're simply perpetuating an old myth that some-
how a feeling of love wafted over you until suddenly a
breeze took it away. And boom—there you are, unloved
and loveless, dripping tears onto your pillow.

Personally, I have dripped plenty of tears onto my pillow,
and as a semi-wise woman of uncertain age, married
and divorced, and having had lovers as well, I finally see
some sunlight at the end of the relationship tunnel.
What is distilled here in easy-to-understand language is the
result of my own suffering and joy, of thousands of men
and women whom I have counseled, as well as the dozens
of friends who have rung me up hysterically at 3:00 A.M.
to tell me "the relationship is over . . ."
I hear it every day and so do you.
"Love is a mystery."
"Relationships don't last."
"There was nothing we could do about it."
Amazing, I thought, how we blame our disasters on fate.

And each time I heard the refrain, "If only there were some way we could work to make it right."

Yet just as often I heard, "But I don't want to *work* at a relationship."

I remember a client of mine, a short, slim, and attractive young woman named Diana, with dark, naturally curly hair, wailed that line into my ear.

"Tough luck," I answered. "Do you work at your job?"

"Yes."

"Do you work to keep your apartment clean?"

"Of course."

"Do you have to put oil into your car regularly?"

"Sure."

"Then why in heavens would you expect the most important aspect of your life, your relationship, to simply run without oil, without tender care, without some work?"

It's ridiculous!

Your garden needs tending, your home, your body, your teeth, *and* your relationship.

But I could see that even though she agreed it would take work, she didn't know where to begin. Strange—we know how to tend a garden. We know how to maintain a car. And many of us know that love is not just a feeling that wafted over us and then was swept away by a sudden breeze.

The problem is that these days WE DON'T KNOW HOW TO TEND A RELATIONSHIP.

Our parents gave us some advice—most of it no longer applies.

Our friends don't seem to know much more than we do.

Almost everyone we meet is having trouble with their relationship.

And the so-called experts seem to be the last place to look
for answers to a problem as complex as how to be in love
without losing sooner or later.
For the longest time I also had no idea how to tend to a
relationship.
I thought I had to shut up every time I was angry.
I thought I was a failure every time I didn't do what my
partner expected.
I spent years blaming my parents and my childhood because
I wasn't happy.
I never knew how to combine a career with a relationship
successfully.
And no matter what I tried it never seemed to work.

Yet during all those years when I was trying to make my relationships work (in the old-fashioned way) a new world
was emerging. The 1960s, the sexual revolution, the
women's movement, and the human potential movement
were laughable at times, but when you sift through all the
experiments and dramatic events of the past twenty years,
something has changed.
Something is different and you ought to know about it.

That young woman I was counseling had been married four
times by the age of thirty-two. That may seem strange to
you, but you can't say Diana hadn't been looking.
Each time she would look "out there" for her happiness, as
though the next man had all the qualities of Santa Claus.
Each time she ended a relationship, she was sure the next
man was going to be "the one," as if Prince Charmings
grew on trees.
Her first husband was short. The second was tall. One was
like her father. Another was like her mother. One of the
husbands was different from anyone she'd ever known
before.

And she looked up at me with her huge blue eyes and asked plaintively, "What am I doing wrong?"

I took a deep breath. How would I ever begin to explain to her how you tend a relationship for the 1980s?

She was trying to find a relationship in the old-fashioned way—the secure and devoted relationship she thought her parents had (which happened to be a subservient angry woman and a domineering frightened man). She was trying to live her life with a man as her parents had done—but the new awareness and the new freedoms made that impossible.

First it was sexual freedom that posed a threat for her. Then it was the women's movement. Later it was her desire to express her feelings with complete honesty. The last marriage broke up over the fact that neither partner was sure they even wanted to be in a relationship.

While some people have managed to change and grow from the shakeups of the past twenty years, no one to date seems to know how to have a relationship that includes the new freedoms as well as the tenderness, love, and commitment that have always been so valuable.

That's what this book is about.

It's about a new era of relationships in which couples can enjoy many of the "old-fashioned" virtues such as tenderness, commitment, and loyalty (out of choice) while having the new freedoms, including sexual fulfillment, honesty, shared power, and equality, and whatever we call our "personal growth."

What I pointed out to my client Diana were the cross-currents that she and everyone today are experiencing. Her head was filled with all the new ideas of the "Me Generation" (or the "Me First" generation, depending on how you look at it), while her heart longed for the stability and romance she imagined as a child. She was upset by what she saw as the inability of the "Me First" generation to have long-lasting commitments, but she also remembered vividly that commitment for her mother had meant capitulating to her father with an angry "Yes, dear" every night for thirty years.

To my own surprise, I assured my client that she could have it both ways—the romance and "love is forever" of the Fred Astaire/Ginger Rogers era as well as the ability to be her own person and not hide behind an image or a role.
I could see she didn't believe me. She didn't think she could have it all—the honesty of being a full human being with the magic of a lasting romance.
Her greatest fear was that love was too ethereal and unpredictable to ever allow her to have what she wanted.

The reason I want to throttle Gordon Lightfoot for his "The feeling's gone and I just can't get it back" is because we and we alone are totally responsible for creating and maintaining love in our lives. It's not something that comes and goes like a strong wind over which we have no control.
In this new era of relationships, each one of us has power and control. Not manipulative control, but real control.
So when the feeling's gone, you need to find out why.
The feeling doesn't have to go unless you say so.
And you *can* get it back whenever you wish.

You probably don't believe that what I'm saying is true.
After all, it's never happened to you. You've heard of a few relationships where both partners were able to be fulfilled and complete. Yet it seems to be some special mystery.
In every generation there are a few "lucky" people who by some natural, intuitive brilliance carve a path of joy and balance, of love and tenderness, and of openly expressed

anger and passion. It seems so rare that we call these people the "lucky few."

But you can have what the lucky few have simply by following the 40-Day Plan whether you have a partner right now or not. And enjoyably discovering what fun it can be to tend a relationship in which you nurture not only your love for another but your growth as an individual.

If you're not in a relationship and you follow the 40-Day Plan, you'll not only be more likely to find a successful relationship, but to tend the relationship in a new way that brings out the best in both of you.

If you are in a relationship now, and you know you're having more ups and downs than you can tolerate (or you're upset about your arguments and dissatisfactions), just ten to twenty minutes a day can transform your relationship.

And yet I'm sure the negative voice inside of you is saying, "It may work for *others*, but will it work for *me*?"

It will work for you if you'll use it to unravel and come to grips with the anger and upsets you've stuffed down your whole life.

It will work for you if you stop blaming your parents for your bad deal in life.

It will work for you if you stop resenting your last partner who is still in your thoughts and feelings.

It will work if you finally decide that you are a loving person no matter what negative and fearful thoughts run through your mind every hour, every minute, and every second (because negative and fearful thoughts go through everyone's mind—including my own).

Some of the lessons and exercises will seem strange to you at first. But remember when you first learned to drive a car? It took a while, with each new lesson feeling uncomfortable in the beginning. Once you mastered the new skills, they became second nature. There are relationship skills in the 40-Day Plan that are new and unique—this book will make them second nature for you.

You will do yourself a disservice if you avoid, judge, or second-guess the lessons and exercises. They are each there for a purpose and each for your benefit. If you follow the instructions and dig deep into your emotions for the truth about yourself and the relationship you want to have, this 40-Day Plan will work for you.

And you will know all that you need to know to have your relationship exactly the way you want it.

During one of our sessions together, Diana told me in absolute despair, "I don't want to spend my life alone. I can't go on getting married and divorced. People think I'm crazy but I know what I want. I want to love and be loved and have a love that lasts."

She asked, "Adelaide, what can I do?"

I then suggested, "If you could have exactly what you wanted in a relationship, what would it be?"

Her silly smirk was gone. She looked me straight in the eye and her voice was clear.

"I want to be myself. That's the one thing I've never been in a relationship.

"When I'm angry I want to be angry. When I'm afraid, I'll be afraid. Turned on when I feel it . . . and honest when I'm not.

"I don't want another starry-eyed romance that starts out in love and turns to hate and resentment. I've done that number too many times already. I just want to stop hiding and start being appreciated for who I really am."

Together, Diana and I began to explore the specifics of what that means for her. This book is the technique that came from those sessions. It incorporates the most useful insights from dozens of psychotherapies and theorists; it expands on the techniques of hundreds of workshops and seminars; it explores the answers and advice gained from thousands of clients and friends, all trying desperately to build a love that lasts.

By distilling our work and the sum of my experiences and insights into forty days of lessons and exercises, the plan is easy to follow. Each day will reveal a different problem area and propose an additional skill you can take into your relationship.

You want to be your own person and you want to love and be loved in a love that lasts. This book will teach you how and I'm confident it will work for you. Don't forget to follow the instructions and be sure to complete all forty days.

And enjoy it. Remember, you and you alone create the joy, the pain, the anguish, and the delight.

As far as I know, nothing equals or surpasses the quality of loving and being loved—for that reason alone, this Plan is worth every moment you give it.

—Adelaide Bry

San Diego, California

INSTRUCTIONS

This 40-Day Plan is like a diet.

Instead of losing the bad habits that keep you overweight and unhealthy, this Plan will help you *lose the fears, habits, and attitudes* that keep you lonely and dissatisfied with your relationships.

No diet plan can work unless you follow the entire program to overcome your resistance and excuses.

Similarly, *Learning to Love Forever* can teach you more about yourself and your ability to have a fulfilling relationship.

But only if you're *honest, persistent, and willing to succeed.*

(Most people aren't—most people don't even believe they'll ever have a relationship they'll enjoy for a long time.)

If you're not willing to have it work for you, then it won't.

Yet if you've had enough disappointment and heartache for one lifetime, this *simple and easy-to-follow* program will transform the quality of your experience of loving and being loved.

The steps are laid out for you in *forty days of short lessons and challenging exercises.*

There are no complicated theories you won't understand and no questions too difficult to answer.

Instead, this 40-Day Plan will help you build a scrapbook of the delights you can expect in your relationship and eliminate the obstacles that stand in your way.

It is unlike anything you've ever read, heard about, or tried, and will be the most successful path to a lasting relationship you've ever encountered.

To complete the 40-Day Plan you only need to set aside *five to fifteen minutes per day* to read and do the daily lesson and exercise.

If you want to reward yourself and skip a day or two in between some of the lessons, or after one of the five parts, go ahead.
But you *owe it to yourself to complete the 40-Day Plan.*

Why? *Because it works!*
It can be enjoyable and fun if you let it,
More challenging and personalized than any class, home-study, or self-help book you've ever used.

In addition, you will find that some of the lessons and exercises are so important and thought-provoking for your particular relationship, you will want to *refer back* to them over and over again after you have completed all forty days.

For some people, the 40-Day Plan is a perfect way to train your mind *in solitude* in order to *prepare* for a loving relationship.
For others, the 40-Day Plan can be done *with your partner—* each lesson and exercise will help your relationship expand and grow.
But whether you do this alone or with a partner doesn't matter—the lessons and exercises are designed to bring out *your values, your feelings, and your preferences.*
No two people will ever have the same reactions, insights, and changes from this Plan.

Note:

There has been a concerted effort made to develop the Plan so that it works for *young and old, males and females, gays and straights,* without losing any of its effectiveness.

Every question and lesson, in some way, applies *specifically to you and your relationship.*

On every one of the forty days, you can have a *major break-through* that will change and improve the quality of your relationship and make love and loving so wonderful that every day can be fulfilling *regardless of the external circumstances in your life.*

PART *One*

[DAYS *1–8*]

DO YOU REALLY WANT
A RELATIONSHIP?

*Before you begin to unravel the obstacles that stand
in your way,
And before you can master the skills for having a
love that lasts,
There is a fundamental question that you and you alone
must answer:
DO YOU REALLY WANT A RELATIONSHIP?*

*You might want a solitary trip around the world or a
"wild and crazy" series of one-night stands.
You might want to spend the next two years fixing up
your car or working on your figure.
Who knows, you might be completely devoted to feeling
disappointed and lonely.*

*It's a waste of time to work at a relationship when you
have no desire to build a love that lasts.
So the first section of the 40-Day Plan lets you look at your
motives and willingness to have it all.
You may find it's not black and white for you—you want
one and you don't want one.
But first you have to be honest with yourself.*

DAY 1

The most profitless thing to
manufacture is excuses.

—B. C. FORBES

Who'd Be Angry If You Were Having a Good Time?

For most of us, relationships are filled with effort, anxiety, compromise, and disappointment.

This 40-Day Plan will give you an alternative method that avoids the traditional traps that have made loving so difficult for so many for so long.

But—are you willing to have love work for you?

If you were having a wonderful time in an ideal relationship, would you lose all your friends?

Would your ex-lover hate your guts?

Would your parents or cousins be jealous?

Most important, would having it all blow your image of who you are?

Would it be too much to ask for you to give up the familiarity of the confusion and disappointment you've been living with?

Would it be too much of a happy shock to your system to wake up each morning knowing that you're in love and that someone shares your love?

This 40-Day Plan threatens every self-defeating idea you've had about love and relationships.

It actually helps you to make your life wonderful every day.

If that's too upsetting to you or to someone whose opinion you value more than your own happiness,

You may want to put the book aside until you're ready for it.

Otherwise, you might die from missing your old, dissatisfied self.

Who'd Be Angry If You Were Having a Good Time?

· Make a list of everyone who would be disappointed or angry if you had a perfect relationship.
(If you fear detection, you can use a *separate sheet of paper* for the people on your list of disapprovers).

_____   _____
_____   _____
_____   _____
_____   _____
_____   _____

· Ask yourself why you let them and their opinions run your life.

· Are you willing to surpass their expectations for you?

· Did you put your own name on the list?

· Are you the person who is secretly sabotaging yourself?

DAY 2

Love casts out fear; but conversely,
fear casts out love.

—ALDOUS HUXLEY

What Are You So Afraid Of?

Let's face facts—
Statistics and everyone you know say the same thing,
"Relationships don't last."

Every one of us has had a broken heart or a shattered dream.
Every one of us has a bad memory of feeling unloved or unwanted.
Every one of us is vulnerable when it comes to loving.

Yet this 40-Day Plan is encouraging you to feel safe and open
   in your relationship.
Lunacy or a malicious joke?

I assure you I don't want you to get burned.
Even more important, I want you to recognize that you're
   not in danger any longer.
On the contrary, if you truly understand what love is, you
   wouldn't be so terrified.
And unless you stop being so afraid of love,
You'll never even begin to know the kind of relationship
   you're capable of having.
Love is not something "out there" that you have to wait for.
It's not something brought in by the wind, the moon, the
   stars, the stork, or any other foolish idea.
It's not something that you can only feel with the exact and
   perfect "Mr. or Ms. Right."
It's not something that somebody can snatch away from you.
Nor is it something that you have to worry about running
   out of.

8

Your thoughts and your feelings are the storehouse where
  love resides.
Inside you is an abundant and limitless supply of an emotion
  called love.
You've had it forever and you've never lost any of it.
(You only think you have.)

People and situations come and go,
But your capacity to love fully and deeply is with you always.
And no matter how you try to shut it off or cover it up with
  fears and regrets,
You are still the owner and master of an infinite supply of
  the world's most treasured resource.

DAY *2* | EXERCISE

What Are You So Afraid Of?

You're afraid that love will disappear or be stolen away by someone.
Today's exercise will show you that's impossible.

· Find a quiet place to sit and take some deep inhales and exhales to relax.

· Close your eyes and make up a fantasy image of a hazy glow of emotion which surrounds your body. Once you see the glow, you can call it your feelings of love.

—What color are they?
—What shape?
—What do they do?
—Can you see the color and shape change in your mind's eye?

· Take your time until you are able to see, with your eyes closed, the hazy glow that surrounds you. Then with your eyes still closed, imagine these feelings of love flowing out and filling up the entire room you're in,

—Then filling up the entire five-mile area around you,
—Then filling up the entire planet Earth.

· How does it make you feel to see your feelings of love?

· How limitless are they?

DAY 3

Our language has wisely sensed the two
sides of being alone. It has created the
word 'loneliness' to express the pain of
being alone. And it has created the word
'solitude' to express the glory of
being alone.

—PAUL TILLICH

Can You Survive Without a Relationship?

Infants need constant attention or they'd die.
You don't.

A child has to look elsewhere for nourishment and affection
or he or she won't have any.
You don't have that problem anymore.

You *can* survive without a relationship.

Yet to the extent that you believe you need a relationship in
order to survive,
You force your relationship to be something it can't be.
A relationship can never provide you with what you won't
provide for yourself.

No relationship removes all the feelings of desperation, in-
security, and neediness you think it might.
Even the most fulfilling relationship can't turn you into
something you're not.
Most people either don't know this fact or they choose to
ignore it.
Most people would rather hold the relationship responsible
for everything that's wrong in their lives, rather than
admit that they're in charge of their own lives.

Can You Survive Without a Relationship?

· Regardless of whom you're with or attracted to, make a list of the attributes of your *ideal* partner, your absolute dream mate—all the things he or she should be, do, and have.

_____   _____
_____   _____
_____   _____
_____   _____
_____   _____
_____   _____
_____   _____

· Now look at the list you've made.
If these are the qualities you admire and appreciate, how many of them do *you* possess?

· Ask yourself if you are holding back on the person you'd like to become because you're waiting for a relationship or a partner to do it for you.

· Are there some attributes on your list that you should become, do, or have on your own?

DAY 4

Life's under no obligation to give us
what we expect. We take what we get
and are thankful it's no worse than it is.

—MARGARET MITCHELL
Gone With the Wind

What If It Just Doesn't Work?

There's nothing more pathetic than two people who are terrified of being alone holding onto a relationship that isn't working.

There's nothing more frustrating than feeling trapped and alone when you're in a relationship.

There's nothing more painful than two people who love each other and can't communicate with each other.

This 40-Day Plan will not force you to stay in a relationship that should be left behind.

It won't tell you to remain imprisoned when there's a way out.

Yet unlike most popular wisdom of the past decade this 40-Day Plan will show you ways that you can save a relationship and fall in love with the same person over and over again.

Strange as it may seem, one of the most important requirements of a love that lasts

Is for both partners to know that they could survive on their own.

Survival is not the reason for building a love that lasts,

And in most cases, the fear of being alone will destroy an otherwise healthy loving relationship.

Only when you feel complete and whole as a person,

Can you have a relationship in which neither you nor your partner is trying to control, manipulate, or "rip each other off."

Only when you stop being terrified of separation,

Can you have the true security of a love that lasts.

A loving relationship is not two half-empty cups drinking from each other in the vain hope of becoming full.
That's an endlessly losing situation.

A love that lasts is like two full cups, regardless of shape and size, overflowing into each other.
Always complete as individuals and always richer from the sharing.

What If It Just Doesn't Work?

· Either find a photograph of yourself before the age of five or recall a picture of yourself as a very small child.

· Talk directly to the photograph or picture and say the following slowly and lovingly:

> Little person, I know your fears.
> I know your dreams.
>
> I can't promise you everything,
> But I can promise that I'll always support you.
> I'll always comfort you and encourage you.
> I'll always accept and love you.
>
> Trust me that I'll never abandon you.
> Trust me that I'll never harm you.
>
> No matter what, I'll always take care of you.
> No matter what, I'll always love you.

DAY 5

To love is to stop comparing.

—ANONYMOUS

What Are You Going to Lose in Order to Win?

Most people look at everything with two ideas in mind,
"How much is it worth to me?"
and "What do I have to give up to get it?"

Apply that type of thinking to a relationship and you'll
probably take the fun out of being in love.

Most people have the idea that if you want love, you can't
have the other things you want in life.
You think to yourself:
Can I really have love *and* money?
Love *and* independence?
Love *and* excitement?

Has it ever occurred to you that love can be something that
allows all other valued emotions and experiences to
flourish?
Love is the one thing that isn't diminished by its use.
It's the foundation on which you can build your dreams—
not the trade-off you have to sacrifice for.
When you're in a supportive relationship, love is the energy
source, not the energy-sapper.
When you're sharing openly with someone who accepts and
encourages you,
You have the strength and safety from which to challenge
yourself and grow.

Working from the sound basis of a relationship that has trust
and mutual respect,

You'll find that you can have love *and* money,
Love *and* independence,
Love *and* excitement,
As long as you don't convince yourself otherwise.

What Are You Going to Lose in Order to Win?

- Just for the fun of it, let's use conventional either/or "what's in it for me?" thinking and apply it to love.

- For each of the following choices, pick an A or a B. And be honest!

  __A. Multiply by 5 the highest amount of money you ever spent in a year.

  __B. A loving relationship that could last forever.

  __A. Your wildest sexual fantasies one after another.

  __B. A loving relationship that could last forever.

  __A. Your dream house in the most ideal location.

  __B. A loving relationship that could last forever.

  __A. Every career goal you've ever imagined for yourself.

  __B. A loving relationship that could last forever.

  __A. More adoration than Queen Elizabeth as well as privacy and protection.

  __B. A loving relationship that could last forever.

  __A. A trip around the world.

  __B. A loving relationship that could last forever.

  __A. Complete support and obedience to all your wishes from those around you.

  __B. A loving relationship that could last forever.

  __A. Total physical health and longevity.

  __B. A loving relationship that could last forever.

· Count up the number of A's and B's you checked. A's___
  B's___

· If you picked four B's or less:

  Ask yourself whether you're capable of putting in the
  effort, commitment, and creativity necessary to make something intangible like love into a reality for you.
  Do you always settle for what's easily available or are there
  some things you'd be willing to persist at in order to
  achieve?

· If you picked five to eight B's:

  You are either kidding yourself or you place a very high
  value on love.
  Ask yourself if you're willing to have the joys and pleasures
  in addition to love—or are you the kind of person who
  sacrifices everything else for love?

DAY *6*

It's pretty hard to tell what does bring
happiness; poverty and wealth have
both failed.

—KIM HUBBARD

What's a Relationship Good for Anyway?

It's been said that love can't pay the bills.
Nor does it mow the lawn or change the diapers.
I doubt love could be trusted to brush your teeth twice a
  day either.

However, love is and always will be the most valuable gift
  in the world.
Even in times of inflation, its worth is far more than money.

You may say, based on your experience, that love is overrated.
You may also fear that it's not stable—like the dollar its value
  fluctuates,
And makes your life shaky and insecure.

Let's assume for a moment that you don't know the first
  thing about love.
Nothing that you've experienced or thought about even
  comes close to the richness of feeling you're capable of
  knowing.
You have nothing with which to compare it.
Are you willing to be open-minded about something you've
  never experienced?
Can you be patient and persistent for something you can't
  measure or compare to anything?
Can you trust your instincts enough to create something unlike anything you've ever known?

That's the mission you're on when you seek to build a love
  that lasts.

No one said it was going to be easy or immediately gratifying.
And the odds are all stacked against you.

You can take on the challenge and do it right this time.
Or you can settle for what keeps you dissatisfied and unful-
filled.
The choice is yours.

What's a Relationship Good for Anyway?

As in the exercise on Day Two, today's exercise will allow you to begin to visualize a form of love. The more you are able to visualize your feelings of love and make them real, the less fearful and threatened you'll be during the times in your relationship when patience and persistence are called for.

· For one whole day, you are going to relate to people in a totally unique manner. Experiment with this exercise on as many or as few people as you want, but make sure to notice the way you feel when you're successfully carrying out the instructions of this exercise.

· Looking at a person who is within your eyesight, ignore for a moment all the physical characteristics about the person. Ignore as best you can all the ideas, judgments, opinions, and thoughts you have about who that person is.

· Instead, look for the spirit qualities emanating from that person. See if you can find the glow that surrounds that person. In addition, extend the glow from inside your mind's eye to surround the person.

· Without telling them what you're doing or making an issue of it, notice the love that seems to be a part of that person. Regardless of what the person is doing, see if you can focus on the love and the hazy glow that exists in the space between you and that person.

DAY

"I did that," says my memory. "I could
not have done that," says my pride, and
remains inexorable. Eventually— the
memory yields.

—NIETZSCHE

DAY 7 | LESSON

Does Love Bring Out the Best or the Worst in You?

Why is it that we sometimes hurt the ones we love?

Have you ever noticed how polite and thoughtful you are when you first meet "the one" and how insensitive you become with "the one" after you've been living with him or her for a long time?

How is it that we're tolerant of the eccentricity and craziness of everyone except the person we say we're in love with?

The answer is that we're often controlled by our fears rather than by our feelings of love.

In the beginning, the fear of making a fool of yourself tells you to put on the best face you can show.

Later, when you're no longer trying to impress, everything your partner does seems to threaten you.

We all become far more monstrous and awful than we really are.

The answer is not to go back to the polite but phony show you put on at the beginning.

Nor do you want to ignore the difficult sides of your personality that get aroused in a relationship.

The trick is to uncover your fears,

And learn to express them without making a mess of your relationship.

The first step toward mastering your fears,

Is admitting you have them.

Unless you're able to see your fears and know they're there,

You'll spend all your time and energy denying them, stuffing them down, reacting to them when they come up, and being overwhelmed by their volatility.

If you're willing to laugh at your fears, you'll find them to be the most humorous parts of your personality.
They have the power to make you run from the things you want,
To destroy the things you have.
And make you into a total fool at the worst possible moments.

On the other hand, when you understand and embrace your fears,
They become just another quirk that makes you unique,
Or another obstacle which you can learn to overcome.

Does Love Bring Out the Best or the
Worst in You?

· What was the most awful thing you ever did to a loved one?

_____

_____

_____

What was the fear that made you do it?

_____

_____

_____

· What was the most awful thing a loved one ever did to you?

_____

_____

_____

What was the fear that made him or her do it?

_____

_____

_____

DAY 8

About risks and mistakes:
Elbert Hubbard defines the word "if" as
a tightrope that stretches from
"but" to "but."

George Bernard Shaw said, "A life spent
in making mistakes is not only more
honourable, but more useful than a life
spent in doing nothing."

Judith Stern called "experience" a
"comb life gives you after you lose
your hair."

Finally, a friend of mine once offered,
"If . . . if my grandmother had balls,
she'd have been my grandfather."

How Many Chances Do You Get in One Lifetime?

Most people fall into one of two groups,
Those who walk around regretting a past mistake,
And those who dread making a mistake in the future.

Some people worry about both.

Most people believe that true love comes only once in a
  lifetime
(If at all),
And that if you miss your boat the first time you don't get a
  second chance.

That's great for soap operas and romantic novels,
But it happens to be pure baloney.

With over four billion people on the planet,
Do you think there might be two or three or maybe even
  ten people you could enjoy meeting, growing with, and
  sharing your life with?
All it takes is finding one of them and not using your old
  habits and fears to destroy the relationship.

It doesn't matter that you got together for the wrong reasons.
It doesn't matter that the person doesn't fit the mold of your
  "Mr. or Ms. Right."
It doesn't matter if you don't hear bells ringing or see fire-
  works.

Love is a lot more subtle than you've been led to believe.

You can resign and retire based on the mistake you made once.
Or make up your mind you'll never get it right.

But that would be a shame, wouldn't it?
Especially since it's day eight and you have no idea what wonders are in store for you.

How Many Chances Do You Get in One Lifetime?

· Have you ever come back from defeat or tried a second time for something that was important to you?

· Make a list of three things in your life that you accomplished after a great deal of persistence and determination. (No matter how trivial they seem now).

_____

_____

_____

· Did you ever think about quitting before you got the end result?
__Yes __No

· Did you ever think you were foolish for sticking to it so long?
__Yes __No

· Did you ever regret the fact that you stayed with it and accomplished what you set out to accomplish?
__Yes __No

REVIEW OF PART *One*

DO YOU REALLY WANT

A RELATIONSHIP?

The first eight days of lessons have uncovered a great deal
about your ideas on relationships,
Your past history in relationships,
And your expectations for a relationship.

Now the time has come to answer the simple question posed
at the start, DO YOU REALLY WANT A RELATION-
SHIP?

If the answer is no, put the 40-Day Plan aside until you're
ready to say yes.

If the answer is yes, then you should begin to notice that
your desire for a relationship comes with a number of old
habits, false expectations, and secret sabotage attitudes that
can keep you from building a love that lasts.

Don't worry.
The remaining thirty-two days will give you the insights and
skills to overcome the obstacles that are in your way.
So when you're ready, go on to Part Two.
And remember to be honest with yourself to gain the maxi-
mum benefit from the 40-Day Plan.

PART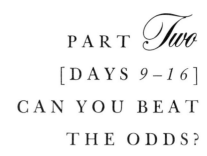

[DAYS *9 – 1 6*]

CAN YOU BEAT

THE ODDS?

The risks are higher than most investments.
The rewards are greater than winning a sweepstakes.

And so we play the game of love.
But how do you win?
Is it a mystery or a stroke of luck?
Or is it something that you can create and build by your
own efforts and abilities?

I believe that it's a little of both, yet the winning difference
is in your power.
There are ways for you to take charge and defy the odds.
There are unique qualities you have that will make
the difference.

Whether you put them to use or become another
disappointed statistic is up to you.

DAY *9*

Creative minds always have been known
to survive any kind of bad training.

—ANNA FREUD

How Not to Duplicate Your Parents' Mistakes

You probably learned most of what you know about rela-
tionships,
From watching your parents' relationship,
And listening to their advice.

The good news is that no matter how hard you try to be like
your parents,
Or try not to be like your parents . . .
You are not your mother,
And you are not your father,
And you don't have to repeat their mistakes.

There may be some influences from your parents that you
find useful,
And others that make you cringe.
But you're the person who decides which influences to choose
and which to discard.

It's not your job to make your parents right or wrong.
It's not the time to work out the conflicts they were never
able to resolve.
Nor is it your responsibility to suffer or limit yourself to
please, pardon, or punish your parents.

The more you try to unravel and relive your parents' lives
for them,
The less you'll be living your own life.

In order to stop chasing after your parents' approval,

Or being wiped out by their disapproval,
You have to do the one thing that most people never do—

You have to let your parents retire as parents,
And become your close friends with whom you once lived
    and shared many intimate times.

You have to become your own nurturing parent and your
    own decisive and directed parent,
Or else you'll never be in charge of your own life.

How Not to Duplicate Your Parents' Mistakes

· List three aspects of your parents' relationship with each other that you'd like to have in your relationship.

_____

_____

_____

· List three aspects of your parents' relationship that you can't stand or that don't work for you.

_____

_____

_____

· List five other relationships you've seen and some aspect of each relationship that you think would work well for you.

Names   **Positive Aspect of Their Relationship**

_____   _____

_____   _____

_____   _____

_____   _____

_____   _____

DAY

I recalled not being able to perform with
a sexy date . . . because some vague twist
of her head reminded me of my
Aunt Rifka.

—WOODY ALLEN

How to Love and Hate the Same Person

A lot of people in relationships have one foot out the door,
And the other on a banana peel.

They're always asking the same basic question,
"Should we/shouldn't we stay together?"

It's not that they don't love each other.
It's just that they hate each other as well.

The reason we love and hate the same person is because the same things that attract us to someone also turn us off to them.
For instance, you meet someone who's just like the parent you're most attracted to.
There's an immediate familiarity and comfort with that person.
But at some point the person acts a little too much like your parent.
And your love turns to hate.

Or you meet someone who's just like your brother or sister.
Immediately the two of you get along wonderfully.
Then later on, when you're living together, you find yourself just as competitive and vicious as you were toward your brother or sister.
And you hate the person who reminds you of them.

Or you meet someone who has the same characteristics as you do.

46

You think you've found your perfect mate.

But then the person does something that makes you see the part of yourself you can't stand.

And you don't want to have anything to do with him or her anymore.

Once you recognize that you're most comfortable with what you're most familiar with,

And you're most impatient with those who are most like yourself and your family,

You can stop viewing love and attraction as a dangerous mystery.

It's a little bit comical and a little bit crazy.

But it happens to be the way we work,

So you'd better start noticing all the ways you take out your feelings about yourself and your family

On your poor, innocent partner.

How to Love and Hate the Same Person

This is an exercise for you to memorize.
Use it whenever it comes in handy.

· Every time you feel yourself go cold and turn off toward
someone you usually enjoy,
And every time you get furious and feel like blaming the
person you're with,
Do the following:

1. Ask yourself what that person is doing that reminds you of:
   your mother,
   your father,
   your brothers and/or sisters,
   your ex-lover,
   or a part of yourself you can't stand.
2. Look into the person's eyes and repeat to yourself silently:
   This person is not my _____.
   (Fill in the blank—mother, father, brother, sister, ex-lover,
   or part of me I can't stand.)
3. Take a deep breath and let it out.
4. Repeat the exercise over and over again until you see your
   partner in front of you and not some person from your past.

DAY

Hatred is a greater tie than love.
The person we hate occupies our mind
far more than the person we love.

—JACOB KLATZKIN

Forgiveness is the fragrance the violet
sheds on the heel that has crushed it.

—MARK TWAIN

Hate the sin and love the sinner.

—GANDHI

Can You Get Even or Just Odder?

Everyone has felt wronged at one time or another.
Some get over injustice.
Others carry it around as a grudge forever.
Guess who lives longer and has a better life?

There are people in your past you would rather not have to
   think about or deal with.
There are old painful memories just below the surface of
   your emotions.
There are unresolved feelings about certain people.
There are things left unsaid.

How can you be open to love someone,
When you're harboring resentments from the past?

How can you feel safe with your current partner,
When you're still afraid to complete the old relationship?

How can you be free to enjoy your love today,
When your thoughts are so easily infiltrated by the past?

Can You Get Even or Just Odder?

· Make a list of all the people in your past or present for whom you are still carrying around feelings of anger, hurt, resentment, or things you've never felt comfortable to say:

_____   _____   _____

_____   _____   _____

_____   _____   _____

_____   _____   _____

· For each person, sit down and write the most honest letter you can. Tell them exactly how you feel about them.
Admit the hurts and describe the anger.
Since you're *not* (under any circumstances) going to send the letter, don't hold anything back.

· Before you finish and sign each letter, make sure there is nothing left unsaid.
For your own peace of mind, and for the quality of your relationships in the future, guarantee yourself that you're letting it all go this time.

· If you begin to feel love for that person after letting out all the resentment, say so.
If you still can't find a way to love them, admit that, too.

· When you are sure you've said everything that needs to be said, read the letter over once to yourself.

· Then slowly crumple it up.
  Roll it into a ball.
  Squeeze it tightly.
  And burn the letter (please be careful).
  Take a deep breath and let it out, feeling a sense of release.

DAY

The art of progress is to preserve order
amid change and to preserve change
amid order.

—ALFRED NORTH
WHITEHEAD

DAY *12* | LESSON

How Are You Different from All the

Failures Before You?

Some very intelligent, warm, loving, and creative people,
Have come up with some awfully miserable relationships.
I'm hoping you can do better.

The first advantage you have is that you're willing to look
at yourself honestly and deeply.
Most people jump in with both feet and don't understand
why they missed the pool.

The second plus for you is that, by virtue of your participa-
tion in Day Twelve of this 40-Day Plan, you know a love
that lasts requires commitment and persistence.
Most people give up as soon as it gets a little uncomfortable.

The third advantage is that you live in a time when you can
have a perfect relationship, absolutely!
The turbulent experimentation of the past twenty years has
produced some wonderful insights and useful methods,
As well as a windfall profit for divorce lawyers.

This is the first decade of relationships that brings out the
best in both partners.
It's the first decade in which both men and women are aware
of how complex a relationship can be,
And how much both partners require in order to be fulfilled.

You may feel as if you've been through a war or two,
But you know you're a lot wiser from the experience.

54

You may feel overwhelmed by all the shifting values and
trends of the past two decades,
But you're aware of more choices and options than any other
generation.

You may feel that the odds of two people staying together in
love for a long time is far too risky,
But you also have a faint notion that if anyone is going to
succeed, it may as well be you and your partner.

How Are You Different from All the Failures Before You?

· List five ways in which you have broken away from your roots.

How are you different from your parents, your family, and the environment you grew up in?

_____

_____

_____

_____

_____

· List five ways in which you have taken the strengths and best values of your roots with you.

What are the secrets and traditions you acquired from your parents, family, and background that apply to your life and relationship now?

_____

_____

_____

_____

_____

· Think about the following:

Are you using the parts of your roots that work for you and discarding only the values and traditions that don't work for you?

DAY

Any jackass can kick down a barn, but
it takes a good carpenter to build one.

—SAM RAYBURN

What Do You Want in the First Place?

Most people are great at complaining.
But when you ask them what they do want in a relationship,
They say, "I don't know."

Your relationship is like a movie,
And you and your partner are sharing the roles of writer,
    director, producer, and stars.
You make up the scenes.
You create the melodrama, the action, and the tears.
You make it come to life and you get to enjoy the results.

Every day it's time to write the next scene.
If you don't come up with something wonderful,
You'll have to settle for whatever is left over from old scripts.

If you don't give it your best work,
You'll have a flop on your hands,
No matter how much time, money, and effort were invested
    before it went sour.

What Do You Want in the First Place?

• The first thing a screenwriter has to know are the feelings he or she wants to convey. Begin by describing the feelings you want to feel every day in your relationship—not some vague concept at the end of the road, but the day-to-day emotions you want your relationship to have for you.

_____

_____
_____
_____
_____

• The next thing the screenwriter has to list are the action scenes that make up the plot. What are the activities, experiences, goals, and challenges you want to share with your partner?

_____   _____

_____   _____
_____   _____
_____   _____
_____   _____

• Ask yourself honestly:
  Is this the script you want to go out and produce?
  Are you asking for too little or too much?
  Are you willing to put in the time and energy to see it gets produced?

DAY

People are not against you;
they are merely for themselves.

—GENE FOWLER

What Turns You Off?

They repealed the law that said you had to keep your mouth
   shut in a relationship.
Maybe your parents' generation had to brood silently,
But you don't.

You no longer have to endure something that's not working.
You can be creative and change it.

You no longer have to run out and have an affair every time
   you're feeling dissatisfied.
You can ask for what you want and be patient as you and
   your partner work out a solution.

Whether you believe it or not,
Your partner doesn't want you to be unhappy.
Unless you're married to Hitler,
In which case you should get a divorce, quickly.

The longer you wait to say something about what turns
   you off,
The more difficult it will be to say it with love,
And to be heard and understood by your partner.

The two of you are partners,
Building a love that lasts,
And if one partner is holding back valuable information
   about what works and what doesn't work,
It can harm the entire project.

Your partner may not jump for joy
When you tell him or her what you don't like,
But if you're willing to put up with the discomfort that can
    surface when you tell your truth
Then you may find that you can create a relationship
Exactly the way you and your partner want it.

What Turns You Off?

· What's the most important thing you could have changed or said in your relationships but didn't?

_____

_____

· What's the most important thing you could have done or said differently to make your sex life more fulfilling but didn't?

_____

_____

· What's the one thing you've been putting up with for a long time that you'd love to change about the way people treat you?

_____

_____

· What's the one thing about your way of treating people that you know you could improve if you put your mind to it?

_____

_____

DAY

. . . the healthy, the strong individual, is the one who asks for help when he needs it. Whether he's got an abscess on his knee or in his soul.

—RONA BARRETT

Did You Ever Try Asking for What You Want?

How often do you get mad at your partner,
For not anticipating what you want and need?

How often do you pretend you don't have an opinion,
When you know full well how you feel?

How often do you and your partner wind up opposing each
    other by accident,
Because neither of you asked clearly for what you wanted?

Isn't it a shame that two people so in love
Can be so unreliable for each other?

When you ask for what you want,
Your partner can say "no" . . . or "yes."
When you don't ask,
Any one of a thousand things can happen,
Most of them frustrating.

When you take the risk,
And admit what turns you on, what you need, or what you
    prefer,
You let your partner know who you are and what makes you
    happy.
Why would you want to keep that a secret?

Sometimes you have to ask a dozen times before you're heard.
Does it matter so long as you get what you want eventually?

Sometimes you have to listen to your partner say "no" and really mean it.
But before you decide your partner is your enemy,
Find out why the answer is "no,"
And find out what would get a "yes" that you could both enjoy.

The complication comes from the silence,
The reluctance,
The resentment,
And the fear of rejection.
Asking for what you want gets you a single result, "yes" or "no,"
Either one delivered with love.

Did You Ever Try Asking for What You Want?

· Remember that you are the creator of your relationship and that you're writing the script from which you'll produce the best scenes possible.

This exercise will help you find the words and deeds that work best for your wants. The clearer you make them, the more likely you'll be understood. The more you're willing to help others come through for you, the more you'll have it the way you want it.

· What do you want your partner to say to you when you're upset?

_____

_____

_____

_____

· What makes you feel loved and appreciated by your partner?

_____

_____

_____

_____

· When are you most vulnerable and most in need of special attention and tender loving care from your partner?

_____

_____

_____

_____

· What makes you feel sexually satisfied with a partner?

_____

_____

_____

_____

· Now that you know the words and deeds that you need to ask for, can you ask for them?

__Yes __No   If no, why not?

DAY

Neither man nor woman . . . can be
worth anything until they have
discovered that they are fools. . . . The
sooner the discovery is made the better,
as there is more time and power for
taking advantage of it.

—LORD MELBOURNE

Can You Avoid Being a Fool?

If you want your relationship to work,
You're going to have to let it go through changes.
Ups and downs.
War and peace.

You may have to feel ignorant and confused once in a while.
You may be shocked and surprised a few times.
You may feel more insecure than you've ever felt as you climb
to the edge of a precipice from time to time.
And certainly you'll feel like a fool and fall on your face once
or twice.
So what!
It comes with the territory.

You've taken risks before.
And you've seen ambitious dreams come true.
You've known the weather to change violently in a matter
of minutes.
And for your moods and emotions to come and go faster than
your explanations can make sense of them.

The only danger is that you'll try to make your relationship
stand still.

By playing it safe and living in the past,
Some people spend a lot of time and effort trying to recapture
something that was once.
That one sexual triumph.

PART *Three*

[D A Y S *1 7 – 2 4*]

H O W   I S   A   C O M M I T M E N T
D I F F E R E N T   F R O M   A
P R I S O N   S E N T E N C E ?

The hardest thing for members of our "Me Generation"
is to make commitments.
Relationships that used to last five decades now break up
after five months.
"True love" seems to last a year.
And everyone seems to be exiting, entering, looking to exit,
or looking to enter a relationship.

Almost none will admit to being happy where they are.
Yet the 40-Day Plan is for a love that lasts.
And the ability to fall in love with the same person over
and over again.

Part Three will provide you with specific tools and insights
to create a loving commitment.
Not one that entraps or limits you.
But one that gives you the freedom to build a relationship
that uncorks your highest self and the best aspects of
your partner as well.

DAY

The only difference between a rut
and a grave is their dimensions.

—ELLEN GLASGOW

Who's Cramping Your Style?

Have you ever noticed that some of your friends change when
they "settle down" into a relationship?
They're often a little duller,
and a lot less likely to be the mischievous, fun-loving people
you used to enjoy.

Then one day you find they've moved out and the relation-
ship is over.
All of a sudden the fun-loving personality reemerges.
Your friend starts exploring new interests and tastes.
Pretty soon he or she is like a whole new person,
And says things like, "I feel like myself again."

Why do some people stop growing as individuals when they
enter a relationship?
Why do you feel a relationship will cramp your style?
And how can you make sure it won't?

The answer lies in your ability to use the relationship as a
source of personal growth,
Not as the end of your development.

A relationship is a safe place for you to experiment with new
ideas, plans, goals, and achievements.
It gives you the stability of love and trust as the basis for
going out into the world.
It's not a prison, but a laboratory for testing out who you
are and who you want to be.
It's not a place to shut off your dreams, but to fuel them.

If you notice at any time that you hold back on your strengths and pleasures,

Or that you're constantly demanding that your partner cut back on the things that make him or her unique,

Then you may be one of those who's using the relationship as a trap where both of you have to become the exact same person.

Not only is it impossible to turn two separate people into one lifeless machine,

But eventually you'll both start hating each other for it.

Who's Cramping Your Style?

· Make a list of the five compromises you've made in a relationship (include any things, activities, friendships, or ideas you had to give up):

	Holdback	Trivial
_____	_____	_____
_____	_____	_____
_____	_____	_____
_____	_____	_____
_____	_____	_____

· Next to each compromise, put a check mark under one of the two columns:

Holdback: Did it force you to hold back on an *important* aspect of who you are and what your dreams are in life?

Trivial: Was it something that helped the relationship but wasn't really central to who you are and what your dreams are?

· Looking back on your list of compromises,

—If you found that most of your compromises were *holdbacks,* ask yourself why you create relationships that are so different from who you are and what makes you fulfilled. Don't you deserve a relationship that will help you live up to your dreams?

—If you found that most of your compromises were *trivial,* ask yourself if you and your partner tend to make things the same for both of you. Are you sacrificing more than you need to? Are you and your partner stifling the things that make you unique?

DAY

Most people resemble great deserted palaces: The owner occupies only a few rooms and has closed off wings where he or she never ventures.

—FRANÇOIS MAURIAC

Do You Want a Partner or a Parent?

If you're looking for a nurturing, selfless, and devoted mate
who jumps at your every beck and call,
Then you should put in a classified ad for a mother, not a
lover.
If you're looking for a mate to buy you things, indulge you
in all your moods and whims, and never show any in-
securities,
Then you're looking for a Santa Claus or a Sugar Daddy, not
a loving partner with whom you can share and grow.

Today, both men and women are changing their traditional
roles at the same time.
Men are learning to say, "I need you" and "I'm afraid."
Women are learning to say, "I'm my own person" and "I
have a path of my own to follow."
Your partner is not going to play the same roles your parents
played for you.
Nor is it likely the two of you will find it easy to understand
each other all the time.
One minute you feel like conquering the world and the next
minute you want someone to take care of you.

Yet if you're still looking for the mom and dad you never
quite had as a kid,
Then you'll either imprison your partner in a role he or
she can never perform to your satisfaction,
Or you'll be disappointed and alone when your partner
leaves you to become a whole person again.

The volatile times we live in don't mean love and relationships can't change and grow with the times.
If you're perceptive, you'll see when you or your partner are asking for a parent,
And you may choose to be the "good parent" at those moments.

Yet for the most part, you'll stop playing the roles that worked so well in the 1950s, but don't work today.
And stop being so threatened when your partner chooses not to be your parent-in-residence,
Because today you and your partner are both capable of so much more.

Do You Want a Partner or a Parent?

· Based on your idea of what is traditionally viewed as "male" and "female" sex roles
(Men and women should answer both questions),
Make a list of ten favorable "male" traits you have that make it unnecessary for you to go looking for a "father figure" to take care of you.

_____	_____
_____	_____
_____	_____
_____	_____
_____	_____

Make a list of ten favorable "female" traits you have that make it unnecessary for you to go looking for a "mother figure" to take care of you.

_____	_____
_____	_____
_____	_____
_____	_____
_____	_____

DAY

If you pick up a starving dog and make
him prosperous, he will not bite you;
that is the principal difference between
a dog and a person.

—MARK TWAIN

Do You Give More than You Receive?

Can you give without resenting your partner?
Can you receive without resenting your partner?
Most people can't.

Some people give in such a way that it smothers.
Others take without believing they deserve it.

Others give only to get in return.
Or take without ever being satisfied.
These people aren't in love—they're at war.

There are three key thoughts that can end the frustrations
   and confusion about giving and receiving.
The first, which the 40-Day Plan has mentioned before, is
   that a loving relationship is not based on scarcity.
You and your partner have more than enough love and gifts
   to share with each other,
Without any threat of running out.
So for God's sake, relax.

The second key thought is that timing is unimportant.
If you extend yourself to your partner today, does it really
   matter if your partner goes all out for you in a week, a
   month, or a year?
Most people want everything to be tit-for-tat immediately.
Of course you don't want a huge imbalance to build up
   between you.
But you also don't need to spend your time measuring, comparing, and trying to keep score.

The third key thought is that you shouldn't expect your partner to be telepathic.

If you want or need something, ask for it.

If you're feeling generous and loving, share it with your partner.

Pretty soon the flow of giving and receiving will be beyond your expectations.

When two people are giving and receiving near their potential, they're both having too much fun to even think about keeping score.

Do You Give More than You Receive?

· List five gifts or special adventures you'd like to give yourself in the next six months.

_____ _____
_____ _____
_____

· List five gifts or special adventures you'd like someone to give you in the next six months.

_____ _____
_____ _____
_____

· List five gifts or special adventures you'd like to share with someone in the next six months.

_____ _____
_____ _____
_____

· List five gifts or special adventures you'd like to give someone in the next six months.

_____ _____
_____ _____
_____

DAY

Jealousy is a way to get rid of
everything you are afraid of losing.

—ANONYMOUS

How Do You Tame the Big Green Monster?

At some point, every relationship has to deal with jealousy.
You can ignore it,
Or try to squash it,
Or make a rule against it,
Or lie about it,
Yet in every case it will come up again even greener than it
    was the first time you felt it.

Even Jimmy Carter lusted in his heart for other women.
So why should you or your partner be free of all desires?

The question is not "What am I missing?" by being com-
    mitted to one partner.
Nor is it "What's wrong with me for being curious?"

The real issue is "What do I want for my primary relation-
    ship?"
And if you and your partner are honest and open in dis-
    cussing what works best for the two of you,
Then you'll establish a trust and a safe method for taming
    the big green monster.

It might be monogamy with open communication about your
    lusts and curiosities.
It might be monogamy and silent desires you know you don't
    need to act out.

It might be an open relationship with shared insights and
    personal growth.

It might be an open relationship with privacy and secrets keeping the primary relationship stable and strong.

You're free to choose.

And to change the well-understood agreement between the two of you after discussing it with each other.

But it's a dangerous monster unless you are certain of your answers to the following:

—Can I be satisfied with just thinking about these other lovers and not acting on my desires?

—Am I doing something I know will hurt my partner or my relationship?

—Can I channel my curiosity about other sexual partners into finding new wonders and pleasures with my primary partner?

—Do I really want an outside affair to consume time and energy with my primary partner?

—Can I handle the jealousy when my partner is having an affair?

How Do You Tame the Big Green Monster?

This exercise will help you see you have more choices than you imagined.

· For one entire day, live inside your fantasies—create in your imagination an affair with anyone you'd like.

· The only rule of the game is that you can't act out. For one entire day, you have to confine all of your lusts and fantasies to your imagination.

· And don't just stop at courtship. Imagine your secret love affair all the way through to its most complete form. Let yourself imagine yourself satisfied and satiated with your fantasy relationship.

· Then take the pleasurable feelings you learned to feel— the insights about yourself and your sensuality—and know you have the power to do it all with the person you love.

DAY

Passion has the power to transform a
human being from a rather limited,
petty, fearful creature to a magnificent
figure reaching at moments the
status of a myth.

—ANAÏS NIN

It's not the men in my life that counts—
it's the life in my men.

—MAE WEST

Whatever Happened to Passion?

Too often the word "commitment" kills the passion in a
   relationship.
You love the courtship and find the security boring.
You're excited by what you can't have and take for granted
   what you do have.

But it doesn't have to be that way.

Passion is an unfolding of the inhibitions we carry around in
   public.
It's going beyond the limited feelings we've had for strangers,
   infatuations, and quick relationships.
Passion is the mystery that doesn't die in a love that lasts.
Rather, the only way to reach your true level of passion and
   intimacy,
Is in a love that lasts.

Have you ever experienced the richness of falling in love
   with the same person for the second time?
Or the third time?
Or the fourth time?
It's no longer a superficial chill from the way he or she looks.
Or a nervous and anxious tiptoe between two strangers.
You no longer have to hold back out of fear of rejection or
   put on a phony image of yourself to impress.

A commitment in a love that lasts is the ticket to letting
   yourself experience more passion, openness, and intimacy
   than you've ever known you were capable of,

And to rid you of all the discomforts of alienation and the
fear of being too honest,
Or of asking for what you want.

Passion should not be confused with the superficialities of
the sexual techniques, the singles bars, and the screen
romances.
Real passion is a world of intimate delights and luscious
trust that very few have ever had the courage to reach for.
Are you going to be one of the few?

Whatever Happened to Passion?

Earlier, in Part One (Day Five and Day Six), you were asked to look at the importance you attach to having a relationship. Here's another chance for you to see whether you really have a desire for the commitment and persistence it takes to build a love that lasts.

· Write down the ten most passionate pleasures in your lifetime (the ten things, activities, or feelings that make you want to live forever):

_____ _____

_____ _____

_____ _____

_____ _____

_____ _____

· Now imagine that they add up to a certain sum. Let's call that sum 100 percent joy.

· Now try to imagine a sum called 1000 percent joy that is the measure of true romantic love between you and your partner. Close your eyes for a moment and visualize yourself with 1000 percent joy.

DAY 22

Some nights he said he was tired, and some nights she said that she wanted to read, and other nights no one said anything.

—JOAN DIDION
Play It As It Lays

What Gets Better with Age?

Most people think sexual desire lessens with age.
Most people think sex gets dull with the same partner.
Most people lose their desire for each other somewhere between three months and three years.

Most people are unimaginative and lazy.

If you were like "most people," you wouldn't have picked up this book or completed twenty-two lessons.
You might think that a wonderful and lasting relationship could be built by anyone—yet you know it's becoming more and more rare.

You know you're creative and persistent.
And you know some unconscious obstacles have been blocking your creativity.
And making your love life less satisfying than it could be.

Your sensuality and sexuality are still mysteries to you.
You still don't know what it is to stop trying to please.
You still don't know what it is to stop making sex fit into the expectations you've been taught by your parents, friends, and social values.
In many ways, you're still a virgin.

In the past, you thought sexuality was about orgasms,
Or power trips,
Or manipulation,
Or duty,

Or habit,
Or necessity.

Only with a long-term partner can you begin to find out what
sensuality and sexuality really are for you.
Only with a long-term partner can you be honest enough
and open enough to find out what you really want to feel,
do, say, and experience.
Only in a love that lasts can you find out what makes you
feel immortal.

There will be a number of other lessons and exercises about
sexuality and sensuality in the 40-Day Plan.
Yet none of them will tell you how to make love.
This will be the first time you've been given the opportunity
to go beyond technique,
And to experience the richness of loving yourself and feeling
all of your emotions in the presence of a loved one,
Which is what sexuality really is.

What Gets Better with Age?

· The first step in experiencing your fullest sensuality is trusting yourself as a sexual being. Today's exercise is a practice session for feeling the erotic power inside you.

· Do it at your own pace and take note of the emotions and insights that occur for you.

· The instructions are simple. Begin by finding a time during the day or night when you can have complete privacy for *at least* fifteen minutes. Lock yourself in a room and remain uninterrupted (possibly with the phones unplugged) as you do the following steps *alone*:

· Very slowly and erotically, take off one article of clothing at a time. This is entirely for your own benefit and it is for you to experience all of your thoughts, feelings, and pleasures with your own body.

· Continue undressing yourself until you are naked. Remember that you are alone and no one can disturb you. Notice all the thoughts that run across your mind and then let them pass without holding onto any of the thoughts. Just continue to make yourself comfortable and relaxed. Allow yourself to feel sensual and warm (with a blanket around you if you are cold) as you rest alone in your nakedness.

· Now begin to touch your body gently and lovingly. Start with your face and shoulders, then move slowly to every part of your body. Notice the smells, tastes, and touch of your skin. Again, letting all your thoughts pass through quickly without holding onto any of them, continue to feel the emotions and increased pleasure as you stroke, caress, and hold yourself.

· Either in bed or some other comfortable place, begin to stimulate yourself but not to the point of orgasm. This exercise is a way for you to learn what turns you on and what makes you feel sensual and loved. For that reason, you are not going to let yourself have an orgasm. If you feel one coming on, take a deep breath and let out the breath. Then slow down, relax, and continue to find the touches and pleasure spots you enjoy the most.

· This process can go on for as long as you'd like, as slowly and goalless as you'd like, with as many "almost orgasms" as you'd like.

· After you are done with the exercise, think about the following:

—Did you enjoy being in control of your sensuality?

—Are you willing to take the insights, inner strength, and clues to your sensuality into your relationship?

DAY 23

The worst sin towards our fellow
creatures is not to hate them, but to be
indifferent to them; that's the essence
of inhumanity.

—GEORGE BERNARD
SHAW

How Do You Teach an Old Relationship

New Tricks?

How can two people, so in love in the beginning, become so
bored with each other over time?

How is it that a relationship can change from a thrill into
an old, worn-out obligation?

People say it's because they grow bored with each other.

But only if you examine the nature of "boredom" can you
understand what that means.

And how to keep it from happening in your relationship.

Boredom can be defined as the absence or the suppression of
excitement and joy.

But in reality it's almost like a festering sore or a pot about
to boil.

It's not just that the excitement is missing.

Rather, it's the fact that there are suppressed hostilities and
resentments forcing the two partners to shut down their
feelings.

And how are two people supposed to love each other or enjoy
each other's company when their feelings are shut down?

No matter what you've been told, boredom doesn't have to
happen in a relationship just because time has passed.

People force themselves to get bored because they won't let
go of the minor irritations and complaints they have with
their partner.

When you don't take out the daily garbage, it begins to pile
up and eventually stands between you and your partner.

It's no wonder you're not turned on to your partner when there's a pile of unspoken garbage just below the surface. Icy looks and hostile silences aren't the result of time passing. You're not really bored—you're mad as hell.

How Do You Teach an Old Relationship New Tricks?

- Today's exercise is only the first step in the creative process you and your partner can do in order to build an exciting and fresh love that lasts. But it is the most critical step, because without it you can't begin to be creative and supportive with each other.

- This is your opportunity to make a list of all the traits, behaviors, quirks, and qualities you can't stand in your current partner (or if you're not in a relationship, use your most recent partner).

- Every opinion, judgment, prejudice, and gripe you've ever had with that person can be listed here, once and for all. No matter how minor or ridiculous it may seem, this is the time to get it all out.

Note: If you want to keep this exercise confidential, then compile your list on a separate sheet of paper and keep it to yourself.

By the way, you may find you need to do this exercise once a year, or once a month, or once a week, or even once a day in order to see beyond the garbage in your relationship.

Now, make your list of complaints:

_____	_____	_____
_____	_____	_____
_____	_____	_____
_____	_____	_____
_____	_____	_____

_____   _____   _____
_____   _____   _____
_____   _____   _____
_____   _____   _____
_____   _____   _____

- Are you sure you've listed them all? If not, go back and add on.

- Now comes the $64,000 question(s):

  —Knowing as much about this person as you do, are you willing to look beyond all the quirks and faults listed above?

  —Can you acknowledge this person for having all these traits and not punish him or her for them?

  —Can you see the love, the creativity, and the specialness of the person?

- Whenever you think you can, write in big letters over the whole page of complaints, "SO WHAT! I LOVE YOU ANYWAY!"

- And remember, this is only the first step in the building process.

DAY 24

It is not fair to ask of others what you
are not willing to do yourself.

—ELEANOR ROOSEVELT

Who's in Charge?

In some societies, men are the boss.

In others, women call the shots.

Quite often, the one who appears to hold the power is really taking orders from the quiet strength of the other.

In the latter part of the twentieth century, in our society, the director's chair is up for grabs.

In some relationships, the two partners jockey competitively for position and eventually both wind up with their own director's chairs—on the balconies of their singles' apartments.

The question is no longer who's in charge,

Because no longer is anyone willing to submit to the rule of another, even a loved one.

Yet the battle goes on.

Even if you think you'd like to give away your power and be taken care of,

Or if you believe you can successfully control and manipulate your partner,

It won't work for very long.

Unless you both share the power, the relationship will be about your struggle and competition for control,

Or your resentment of the inequities in your partnership.

Eventually the two of you will figure out you're both too bright and too creative to sit back and let one of you run the relationship.

Eventually the controlling partner will see it's no fun fighting for power instead of love.
Eventually the two of you will begin to bring out the best in each other.

A love that lasts is the most humane of all partnerships.
Both partners have a vested interest in every decision and choice.
Once you stop trying to give up your power,
Or trying to take away someone else's power,
You'll see how incredibly effective two in love can be.

Who's in Charge?

· Analyzing your relationships
(there are no right or wrong answers—just food for
thought):

	You	Your Part- ner	Both	No- body
Who plans the vacations, travel, and special adventures?	____	____	____	____
Whose schedule dictates when you can be together?	____	____	____	____
Who initiates plans to go out on a Saturday night?	____	____	____	____
Whose mood seems to dominate?	____	____	____	____
Who sees through an argument first and starts to look for a solution that will work for both of you?	____	____	____	____
Who makes the spending decisions?	____	____	____	____
Who says no more of the time?	____	____	____	____
Who brings more problems into the relationship?	____	____	____	____
Who brings in more money?	____	____	____	____
Who talks more?	____	____	____	____
Who gets upset more?	____	____	____	____
Who initiates sex?	____	____	____	____

	You	Your Part-ner	Both	No-body
Who complains more?	——	——	——	——
Who comes up with pleasant surprises?	——	——	——	——
Who has one foot out the door?	——	——	——	——

· Look over your answers to the above questions. Can you spot any one of the following patterns?

1. Are you constantly giving away your power and hoping your partner will make the relationship great for you?
2. Are you constantly putting in time and effort without allowing your partner to share the helm with you?
3. Are you and your partner capable of turning more things into enjoyable joint efforts?
4. Are you and your partner fighting for control?
5. Are you and your partner both afraid to take the initiative to make the relationship the way you both want it?

· Now list three things that you could change or improve to make your creative ideas and energies more active in your relationship:

——————————————————————————
——————————————————————————
——————————————————————————

REVIEW OF PART *Three*

HOW IS A COMMITMENT DIFFERENT FROM A PRISON SENTENCE?

The definitions of the word "commitment" range from
   putting someone in a mental institution to agreeing to
   binding financial obligations.
Yet there is one which best describes the "commitment"
   which applies to a love that lasts.
To commit is to "carry into action deliberately."
In other words, your commitment allows you to make real
   what you were thinking in your mind or feeling in your
   heart.
And it does so deliberately, which means by your own will
   power, creativity, and persistence.

This section helped show you that a loving commitment
   shouldn't entrap or limit you,
But should be a basis for bringing out the best in both
   partners.

How well you carry out that opportunity is up to you,
But you will be helped even more by the insights into communication and romance which follow in the final two
   sections.

PART *Four*

[DAYS 25–32]

COMMUNICATION AND
THE ART OF LOVING

*Everyone would like to have a love that lasts, yet hardly
anyone is able to.
And the breakdown usually comes in the area of
communication.*

*By now, you've admitted that you have resentments and
dislikes,
and a lot of love.
The problem is how to express your love and also be able
to express your anger and irritations.
How do you share with your partner the secrets you've
been keeping inside?*

*The 40-Day Plan, in this fourth section, will give you very
detailed and specific aids to overcome the
communication gaps.
Methods to deal with anger and discomfort.
Words to use to make your partner your ally instead of
your enemy.
And ways to share the good feelings with your partner.*

*Communication skills may be the only thing standing
between you and the relationship you want and deserve.
The secret of love and loving is no longer an impossible
mystery to you.*

DAY 25

Loneliness is never more cruel than
when it is felt in close propinquity with
someone who has ceased to communicate.

—GERMAINE GREER

What's So Sexy About Ears?

Do you know how to listen?
No, not just to sit and wait your turn to speak.
Or sit in judgment and pretended interest.

Do you know how to really listen?
To find the innocence and the beauty hiding behind all the
  words and affectations.
To find the "I need you" behind your partner's stories.
To appreciate the lovable character who's far more colorful
  than the words he or she is using to describe something.

Some therapies and self-help programs teach you the words
  and the acts to perform to make it look like you're there
  for the other person,
That may be great for selling someone an insurance policy,
  but it doesn't work for love.

The 40-Day Plan isn't going to suggest a way to present yourself to make it look like you're listening,
Or a technique to make you focus on what your partner is
  saying.

Listening is much deeper than that.
It's far more sexy and luscious than you've ever known.

Listening is the experience of looking into your partner's
  eyes, when he or she is talking, and feeling a rush of love
  that is totally independent of the words or the topic of
  conversation.
You may even feel a rush of tears welling up in your eyes
  or a sense of relaxation coming over your body when you
  truly listen to your loved one.

What's So Sexy About Ears?

· For one whole day, try an exercise every time someone is talking to you up close.

· Instead of rehearsing in your mind what you're going to say back, focus your attention on the person's eyes.

· Then the speaker's lips.

· Then the laugh lines next to the eyes.

· Then the tiny, vulnerable spot at the corner of the nose where the nostrils meet the cheek.

· Then the eyelashes.

· Then the eyes again.

· Can you see that the person doing the talking is really just a lovable human being with the same fears and dreams you have?

· Regardless of the words, is the person asking for your acknowledgment and support? Are you willing to give it?

DAY

There are worse words than cuss words,
there are words that hurt.

—TILLIE OLSEN
Tell Me a Riddle

Do not use a hatchet to remove a fly
from your friend's forehead.

—CHINESE PROVERB

How to Prevent a Minor Tremor from
Becoming an Earthquake

The toughest lesson for people to learn,
And the one that makes some successful and others failures
  at relationships,
Is the ability to vent your anger and upsets without applying
  blame to your partner,
And not to think the love is gone just because you're angry.
Obviously, the reason you get upset is not just the here-and-
  now incident.
The incident is a pain, but the eruption you begin to feel
  has more to do with some other incident that dates back
  to your childhood,
Or to some small irritations that have been piling up over
  time,
Or to some future situation you're secretly dreading.

The first thing you have to realize is that it's totally appropriate to get angry and upset and fearful and sad.
They repealed the law which said the only emotion you
  could show in a relationship is smiling bliss.
However, the 40-Day Plan will show you a way to see beyond
  the rage to the other side of the hate, where love is always
  waiting for you to get through the upset.

Everyone knows the feeling.
You're perfectly calm and then, all of a sudden, you're feel-
  ing tense, cringing, confused, angry, and trapped.
Do you flee or do you fight?
The adrenaline pumping in your system requires you to do
  one or the other.

Most people make the mistake of believing that the person
   sitting right next to them is the cause of the upset.
They don't even have time to consider that it might be some
   old hurt rearing its ugly head,
Or some fear that's creeping into their mind with a force
   and an urgency that baffles the senses.

It is always safe to assume that you're never ever upset for
   the reason that appears obvious during that first second of
   rage.
You're never correct in assuming that lashing out at your
   partner is going to solve anything.
Knowing, then, that you're angry as hell and you're not
   going to take it anymore, there is a way to express the rage
   without punishing your partner.

How to Prevent a Minor Tremor from

Becoming an Earthquake

Here's a method you can use to express your upsets without shaking up the foundation of your relationship.

· Step 1: When the anger and upset start to well up in you:

—Immediately stop what you're doing and feel the feelings rushing through you.

—You may want to take short inhales and exhales.

—If it's a conducive environment, you may want to make sounds and let your eyes fill with tears, or scream and shout.

—You may want to admit out loud, "I'm really mad."

Regardless of what you do physically, you must remember two things:

1. You're not going to die from feeling the intensity of your anger.
2. You're not going to hurt anyone—you're simply going to go through your anger to the lesson that waits for you on the other side of the feeling.

· Step 2: As the eruption is being expressed by nonverbal breathing, sounds, tears, and movements, you can begin to use your mind again.
Instead of looking for revenge or taking it out on someone else, ask yourself the following:
What fears are being triggered by the incident that started this upset?

What past incident are you reliving?
What future situation are you dreading?
Instead of yelling at your partner or blaming him or her, you can verbalize, with just as much emotion,
"What terrifies me about this is . . ."
"What this reminds me of is . . ."
"What I'm feeling right now is . . ."

- Step 3: As you are beginning to see the real terror and upset that are bigger than the incident that just happened, You will want to enlist your partner's help in being your moral support and listener as you unravel the confused feelings.

  Instead of turning on your partner, you should ask your partner to be patient with you in that moment.

  The two of you become allies in letting you work through the upset and see the clarity about your fears.

  Then the two of you can celebrate when the upset subsides.

DAY

If you don't run so far,
the way back will be shorter.

—THE MIDRASH

Forgotten the lies, the deceit, the sudden
bursts of temper, the vitriolic tongue.
Only the warmth remained, and the
love of living.

—DAPHNE DU MAURIER

What to Do After the Insults Fly

Sometimes the tongue is quicker than the brain.
And the words get hateful and ugly.

You have three choices.
Some people stuff their resentments and wait for them to
    show up ten times stronger at some later date.
Some people run away from each other every time the going
    gets rough.
Some people perform miracles.

The miracle you're going to perform
Is simply the ability to turn war into peace and hate into love.
Certainly it's a talent not too prevalent in today's world.

Some people call the miracle "forgiveness" and others call
    it "letting go."
No matter what you call it, it involves one or both partners
    getting off their stubborn position and finding a way to
    be bigger than the hurt and more human than the petty
    words that were exchanged.
And you might as well be the one to volunteer to go first.

The reason you want to go first in clearing up misunder-
    standings, angry words, and barriers between you and your
    partner is that you are the one who has to take charge.
You're the one who can make your life less stressful and your
    relationship less threatened.
You're the one who can perform the miracle of turning war
    into peace.

The first place to begin is with yourself.

Are you willing to love the other person in spite of what happened?

Or do you want to hold it over your partner's head as an ever-present thorn in your relationship?

Are you willing to admit that you were a bit of an ass?

Or would you rather pretend you were an angel—remembering, however, that angels with wings don't have much fun on earth.

Are you willing to let your relationship have some messy moments and angry moments and volatile moments,

Without making those moments into long-lasting bags of garbage you carry around like a painful burden from then on?

What to Do After the Insults Fly

Here's an exercise for whenever you and your partner are at each other's throats. Or you might use it during that half-second just before you're about to turn a nasty disagreement into an all-out war.

· First, you have to call a twenty-minute "time out." No matter how heated the fight, you have to separate for twenty minutes to cool out.

· Next, go to a safe and quiet place where you can be alone for the twenty minutes. Find a place to sit in peace while the storm passes.

· Close your eyes and let yourself relax and feel comfortable with yourself. This is not the time to be debating what to say or what to do next. It's time for you to feel whole again with all the emotions running through you.

· When you feel your body starting to relax, it's time to close your eyes and visualize you and your partner calling in an imaginary advisor.

· With your eyes closed, visualize an advisor whom you can trust and tell him or her that you love your partner and you want to work through the problem. Tell your advisor that you don't want to hate your partner and you want a solution which can satisfy both of you.

- Then explain the situation and the fight to the advisor (be sure to include how you contributed to the problem as well as your partner's role).

- Ask the advisor what to say and do so that you and your partner can both win.

- After you're relaxed and you have an answer to help you end the fight, go back to your partner and open up the discussion for possible solutions.

- Begin the discussion by admitting your contribution to the problem. Then remind your partner that you want the best for both of you. Then begin to explore possible solutions together.

DAY 28

The great secret of successful marriage
is to treat all disasters as incidents and
none of the incidents as disasters.

—HAROLD NICOLSON

How to Ride the Roller-Coaster

There's one right they left out of the Bill of Rights.
And one mood most people in relationships refuse to acknowledge.

No matter what you've been told in the past,
Or believed about what's appropriate and what's not
For yourself or for your partner,
You both have the *right* to get depressed.

Not every day without end,
But when the "blue funk" hits you or your partner,
It doesn't have to mean a crisis in the relationship.

We each have a variety of moods,
And sometimes they're even and smooth.
Other times they're rough and volatile,
But as on a roller-coaster,
You have to sit back and enjoy the ride.

Trying to stop the moods as they flow through you
Is like trying to get off the roller-coaster too soon.
You'll give yourself or your partner bruises
And feel dizzy and disoriented for days.

When the "blue funk" comes over you or your partner,
Give it a bubble bath or a lunch or an easy chair.
Say "Hello there" to your depression and see what message
it's trying to tell you.

Giving yourself and your partner the right to have ups and
   downs
Speeds up the time the "blue funk" will pass through you.
Love doesn't mean smothering, helping, coaxing, cajoling,
   lecturing, manipulating, or judging.
In fact, unpressured, quiet, supportive love is the fastest cure
   for the mood swings we all have.
And if you can love yourself and your partner during the
   lows, you'll find the highs are even higher.

How to Ride the Roller-Coaster

This four-step exercise will give you a way to turn depressions from dangerous crises into benign learning exercises. For today, pick a time when you're tired, unhappy, worried, or just moody and do the following:

· Step 1: Listen to the Noise Inside Your Head.
  For five minutes you are to do nothing but sit comfortably in a chair and listen to all the thoughts running through your mind. Don't judge, solve, dwell on, or analyze any of them. Just notice how much your brain is making noise. And know that each thought passes freely, always followed by another thought.
  If you let the thoughts pass freely across your mind, you'll begin to feel relaxed and less anxious to act on each negative thought.

· Step 2: Become Independent of the Noise Inside Your Head.
  You've been listening to the thoughts and emotions for five minutes. Say to your brain, "Thank you for sharing," and then make up your mind that you're going to take the next step independently of all the competing demands and anxious emotions you listened to.
  This step is simply a way of your finding out who you are and what matters to you—in spite of all the demands and emotions running through you.

· Step 3: Find Your Center Again.
  Simply by making two lists, you will be able to break free of all the noise inside your head.

The first list is three things that are going right for you and for which you are grateful:

_____

_____

_____

The second list is three things you can look forward to and for which you are enthusiastic:

_____

_____

_____

· Step 4: Refocus Your Attention on What Matters.
You now have a clearer sense of yourself as greater than the problems and worries inside your head. That noise will always be there and sometimes you'll need to act on it—but most times you'll need to find a quiet moment to let all your fears have their say and then go on with the important business of your life— namely feeling gratitude for the things that are going right for you and feeling enthusiastic about the things you're looking forward to.

DAY

True friendship comes when silence
between two people is comfortable.

—DAVE TYSON GENTRY

The language of friendship is not words
but meanings.

—THOREAU

DAY *29* | LESSON

How Not to Abuse Your Companion

Most of our parents were dupes—
Nice people, but easily tricked by us.

Whenever we felt hungry or uncomfortable and complained
loud enough, they felt responsible.
When we cried, they jumped to attention.
And when we blamed them for not doing enough, they
usually felt guilty.
It was all very convenient to have full-time servants called
parents.

To this day, most of us still expect our companions to do
something every time we're hungry or uncomfortable.
And we get cranky and defensive whenever they don't jump
fast enough.

In a relationship, your partner may be your frequent companion, but he or she is not your dupe, your servant, or
your parent.
No matter whether you're taking a long drive together,
sitting in a restaurant together, or waking up next to each
other, you've got to break through the tendency to associ-
ate them with the way you treated your parents.

Most people use their adult minds, their increased ability to
use words as manipulators, and their insights into psychology
To become even more controlling of the people around them
than they were as small children.

Even if it's super-covert and very polite, it still won't help a love that lasts.

No matter how much you might want to turn your companion into the person you can blame,
The person you can depend on to do things you don't want to do for yourself,
The person you want to dominate,
Or the person you want to lash out at every time you feel lousy,
It just won't work.

Your mate deserves better treatment than you gave your parents.
In fact, your mate should demand better treatment than you give yourself.

How Not to Abuse Your Companion

- For one whole day, you're going to notice your mood swings and the changes in your feelings from one moment to another.

- As often as you can remember, notice whether you're up or down,
  Open or defensive,
  Cranky or relaxed,
  Friendly or difficult to be with.

- Everyone has a million mood changes in a single day, so don't think you're strange when you notice how often and how dramatically your feelings shift.

- With each mood, notice whether you're thinking about the past, the present, or the future.

- With each mood, notice how quickly it comes to you and how quickly it leaves when you let it.

- With each mood, think about how foolish it would be to try to place responsibility or blame for the mood on the people or things around you. It's just thoughts and noise inside your head. To try to find an external cause and to place the mood on another person are a lot harder work and takes longer than the mood would stay if you just let it go.

DAY *30*

Shared joys make a friend,
not shared sufferings.

—NIETZSCHE

What Comes After the Gripes?

Some people are always trying to fix things, change things,
Without a moment's peace,
In a constant state of dissatisfaction.

If you're constantly unhappy or unsure with everything in
your life, eventually you'll bring your love of complaining
to your loving relationship,
And no relationship can grow in an atmosphere of gripes and
constant dissatisfaction.
The best you'll ever get is resignation.

It's one thing to cultivate the highest aspects of your partner
and yourself
To see what amazing results it brings to your relationship,
To see how wonderful you can make it when you break free
of your past constraints.

It's another to play the constant critic and always be sure that
wherever you are together,
"It's not good enough."

This applies to sex as well.
If you're always playing the critic, of yourself or your partner,
There will always be an unpleasantness and an anxious effort
attached to your love-making.

If you do your best,
And enjoy yourself in the process,
And marvel at the results you get,

You'll be forever surprised, forever involved, and forever growing and changing.

Your job in a relationship and in your love life is to cultivate and share,
To open up your imagination and try out your visions,
To admit to your fantasies and communicate your most outrageous desires.

A relationship is so easy to criticize and destroy, it's certainly no joy to a full-fledged nay-sayer.
So even if you tend to be the cynic, give your relationship a break.
Look for the beauty in your love of another person.

DAY *30* | EXERCISE

What Comes After the Gripes?

· Try this exercise tonight, alone or with a partner, and then do it once a night, once every few nights, or once a week for as long as you find it useful and enjoyable.

· Repeat the words "Three things that turned out wonderfully today were:

1. _____
2. _____
3. _____ "

(These can be from any aspect of your life.)

· With each one, no matter how trivial or insignificant, feel a sense of completion and satisfaction.

· Then repeat the words "Three good things that may happen tomorrow or very soon are:

1. _____
2. _____
3. _____ "

· With each one, sense your purpose and commitment to making them come true.

· Feel free to share this exercise with your partner as a way to enrich your self-esteem and purposes in life.

DAY

I get such a sense of tingling and vitality
from an evening's talk like that; one's
angularities and obscurities are
smoothed and lit.

—VIRGINIA WOOLF

All I'm gonna say about sex is, "When
you're hot, you're hot—and when
you're not, you're not."

—WERNER ERHARD

The Art of Pillow Talk

A friend of mine says he often has sex in order to get the hugging and closeness that follows.

Another person I know loves the massages that go with lovemaking more than intercourse itself.

Still another argues that sex ought to be the place where people can stop trying to please—instead they can just luxuriate and playfully enjoy a partner who has the same purpose in mind.

Finally, I know someone who never has sex the same way twice, and always with the same partner. It's not that she's into gimmicks and devices, but rather the pace, the touching, and the roles change every time she and her partner get into bed.

And yet most people on most nights go for the orgasm and quit.

Sex is no longer a mystery.

For the past twenty years there have been so many books, courses, seminars, experts, therapies, techniques, and obsessions that whole industries (including books and therapies) have stayed profitable as the gurus of sexuality.

Every rule and inhibition have been questioned and left up to the individuals.

Every variation and technique have been tried, written about, and shown in graphic detail.

For the first time in history, people have been given permission to look, touch, taste, smell, do nothing, relax, hold, cry, laugh, talk, ask, offer, explore, and experiment in bed.

So much has changed and yet so many are still strangers in bed.

You need a little courage to ask for what you want.

You need to be a good listener and a sensitive lover to respond to your partner's secret pleasures.

You need to stop worrying that the relationship lives or dies based on performance in bed.

It doesn't—but it makes a relationship wonderful when the two partners know they can and will be sexually fulfilled with the person they love most.

DAY *31* | EXERCISE

The Art of Pillow Talk

· Making your ideas as specific as possible, list as many
thoughts, feelings, experiences, and physical sensations you
can imagine that you have tried and loved, have thought
about trying and would love, or would just like to try and
see what happens:

_____   _____
_____   _____
_____   _____
_____   _____
_____   _____
_____

· Again, try to be specific, as you write out the ways in which
you think a long-term lover and a love that lasts would
make you more sexually open and more sexually fulfilled.

_____   _____
_____   _____
_____   _____
_____   _____

· Finally, list the ways you would like to be for your long-
term lover that you've never let yourself be before.

_____   _____
_____   _____
_____   _____

DAY *32*

Too much of a good thing
can be wonderful.

—MAE WEST

DAY *32* | LESSON

A Few Kind Words Never Hurt Anyone

Everyone needs strokes.

During courtship and at the beginning of a relationship, the
poems, flowers, words of support and encouragement, and
the excitement of going all out for your lover seem easy
and pleasurable.

After you make "the commitment," your partner gets taken
for granted and domestic drudgery sets in.
Occasionally, you'll stop doubting and criticizing long enough
to give a manipulative piece of encouragement.
Or a flower or kind word to make up after a fight.

What a shame.
What a waste to save all your creative romance and sensual
surprise for people you barely know.
And to ignore or undervalue the constant need for love and
affection in the people you care about most.

Giving strokes needn't be a burden or an effort.
But you may have to learn to change your habit of going all
out for what you can't have and taking for granted what
you do have.
We all do it, but a relationship is so much more wonderful
when we break the habit.
And when we stop expecting something in return.

Once you get into the habit of acknowledging your partner
when he or she looks good,

Expressing your thanks when he or she does something special for you,

Encouraging your partner to face the world and live up to his or her dreams,

And creating an atmosphere in which your partner can trust you want only the best for him or her,

Then your love will grow in ways you never previously imagined it could.

A Few Kind Words Never Hurt Anyone

· Make a list of five things you can do for your loved one in
the next week, month, or six months.

_____

_____

_____

_____

_____

· Make a list of five surprises you'd like to give to other
people in your life . . . things that would make their days.

_____

_____

_____

_____

_____

· Make a list of five ways in which you could be a better
friend to yourself.

_____

_____

_____

_____

_____

The rules about relationships have changed in the past two
decades.
You no longer have to hold it all in,
You no longer have to deny who you are in order to win
someone's approval,
And you no longer have to lie and cover up to keep the relationship going.

The new freedom has been confusing for most and destruc-
tive for many.
Yet for you it provides new opportunities to share with,
respect, and explore the delights of your partner.
The new freedom made many selfish and impatient,
But now it is also the key to showing you how to create a
deeper and more fulfilling love that lasts.

Now that you've completed four sections of the 40-Day Plan,
you can begin to feel accomplished at recognizing many
of the skills that make a loving relationship more than it
ever could be before.
You still have some doubts and discomforts, but there's more
to come in Part Five to increase your chances further.

PART

[D A Y S 3 3 – 4 0]

THE ROMANCE YOU NEVER
THOUGHT YOU COULD HAVE

It's hard to tell travellers what to expect
When they venture to a place they've never seen.

And just as hard to keep them down on the farm,
Once they've seen Paris.

You're exploring new territory for yourself,
And your old expectations and experiences about relation-
ships no longer suffice.

As you complete the final section of the 40-Day Plan,
Notice the nervousness and excitement that comes with
charting a new course,
And mastering a complex forty days of intense learning
and personal growth.
Completing all forty days shows the level of your
commitment,
And you deserve to have the insights and skills work for
you in your daily life.

DAY *33*

A quiet conscience sleeps in thunder
But rest and guilt sleep far asunder.

—BENJAMIN
FRANKLIN
Poor Richard's
Almanac

Did you know you were a great liar?
Since day one you've been covering up your feelings,
Smiling when it hurts,
Saying "yes" when your instincts say "no,"
Saying "no" when you wish you had the guts to say "yes,"
Always finding a reason to trust your head instead of your
    heart.

Your whole life you've learned it's not safe to trust.
You've been lied to and manipulated.
You've learned to put up defenses,
And you're sure they've kept you alive.

Yet now it's time to put down your defenses
With your partner and with yourself.
It's time to build a relationship in which you are safe,
And learn to trust again.

In order to live together and grow together,
You and your partner are going to make agreements—
"I'll do the dishes, you make the bed."
"I'll pay the grocery bill, you call the plumber."
"I'll relax, you be gentle."

Trust is not the blind faith you once thought it was.
It's something you build by keeping your agreements.
And when you need to change an agreement, you do so with
prior verbal communication,
Not with excuses and laments after the fact.

Trust is not the flimsy myth you've found most of your fellow
  liars have made it.
If you're going to make honest agreements
And keep them,
Trust will be the most firm basis imaginable.
And your relationship will flourish in an atmosphere of
  mutual respect.

By the way, being a former liar shouldn't be a handicap
As long as you start to tell the truth.

Whom Can You Trust?

· What's the biggest lie you ever got away with in a relationship?

_____

· Looking back, were there any indirect or hidden problems that resulted from that lie?

_____

_____

_____

· Would you want that lie to happen again in your ideal relationship?
__Yes __No Why or why not? _____

_____

· Are you able to trust yourself that you won't spoil the trust in your relationship?
__Yes __No Why or why not? _____

_____

_____

DAY 34

. . . if I can feel the sun in my eyes
and the rain on my face,
why can't I feel love.

—JOAN
ARMATRADING
"Love and Affection"

Love Ain't Nothing Till You Give It Away

Everyone's waiting for something.
Holding a little back in case someone better comes along.
Keeping the lid on in case it's still not safe to feel the depth
of your feelings.

Some people die never letting themselves give and receive the
love that's waiting for them.

No one is telling you it's easy to build a love that lasts.
You may love and hate the same person.
And shout and scream and sometimes feel completely turned
off to your partner.
But in the very next moment, you could be feeling more
passion and trust than you've ever known.

You have to start by sharing your love,
Remembering that it can never run out.
You have to start by giving it away,
To see what comes back to you.

The worst that can happen is that you'll make a fool of
yourself,
Which we both know you've done before and it didn't kill
you.

Only this time you're going to do it differently.
This time you're going to give your love along with a truer
picture of who you are.
You're going to tell the truth from the start about what you
like and what you don't like.

You're going to do the dance with style and enjoy the script
   you're writing.
And you're going to be honest with yourself about whether
   you're building a love that lasts,
Or just another set of training wheels.

You're the creator and the builder.
And you won't have anything until you build it.
Love ain't nothing till you give it away,
And it comes right back to you.

DAY *34* | EXERCISE

Love Ain't Nothing Till You Give It Away

- You've been living with yourself your entire life. Certainly, there's got to be an attraction.

- Just so you're certain your partner will want to stay with you as long or even longer than you've stayed already:

  Make a list of all the qualities and things you do that make you lovable:

  _____ _____
  _____ _____
  _____ _____
  _____ _____
  _____ _____
  _____ _____
  _____ _____
  _____ _____

DAY *35*

Half the failures in life arise from
pulling in one's horse as he is leaping.

—J. C. AND
A. W. HARE

Can You Recognize a Good Thing?

When twenty things are going right,
And one thing goes wrong,
Are you the kind of person who thinks disaster has struck?

When you and your partner have been sharing and loving
    and growing and enjoying,
And then all of a sudden a dispute arises,
Are you the kind of person who thinks the relationship is
    over?

You've come close to having a good relationship before,
You've felt some of the feelings,
And known some of the delights,
And dreamed about the power of love.

Yet here you are,
Still uncertain,
Still questioning and skeptical,
Still a little bit sad,
That it's not going to happen to you.

Your fears are enough to make you shut off your feelings,
And cover up who you are,
And start lying again about what you want and don't want.

For crying out loud,
Don't let your fears make you blind to the love.
No matter how new and strange and uncertain it feels,
Don't let one little upset throw you off track.

You've come too far and learned too much,
To forget everything in a moment of anger.
You've felt too many strong feelings and known too much of
your capacity for love,
To close off and hide again.

Can You Recognize a Good Thing?

· In order to make sure you don't fall apart when things get rough, it helps to take stock of what's going right in your life. This inventory of your assets should be done as often as you'd like, just so you won't forget that things are not as bad as they seem.

	Right Now	**In the Next 6 Months**
What do you look forward to in your day-to-day routine?	_____	_____
	_____	_____
	_____	
What old habits are you changing for the better?	_____	_____
	_____	
What special projects and adventures are you cooking up?	_____	_____
	_____	_____
	_____	
What physical and intellectual growth steps are you taking?	_____	_____
	_____	_____
	_____	
What new experiences and feelings are you exploring?	_____	_____
	_____	_____
	_____	

DAY

Those who love deeply never grow old;
they may die of old age,
but they die young.

—ANONYMOUS

How Many Moments Are There in a Second?

If you live your life fully in the present moment, it can be abundantly rich.
If you live in the past or the future, it can be hell.

The most powerful argument for a love that lasts
Is that a secure relationship lets both partners
Stop analyzing the past and planning for the future
Long enough to experience the present.

With your partner there can be billions of moments of exploration, growth, and peace
In the matter of a simple minute together.
The two of you can see eternity and the plan of nature
By looking together from separate eyes at a single flower in a single second.

Great and special moments don't take very long in a love that lasts.
Yet when you string them together with your commitment and trust,
They keep happening from the time you wake until the time you go to sleep at night.

There's the special moment of watching your partner still sleeping.
And the newness of turning and seeing your partner looking at you as though he or she has discovered something wonderful about you for the first time.

And the simple pleasures of sharing a meal, taking a long walk, or just thinking about each other.

Each of them heightened by the strong feelings you've let yourself feel in the presence of your partner.

A loving relationship used to be a huge institution with a massive set of rules, structures, and form.

Now it's a series of special moments, shared pleasures, and creative missions together with your partner.

The institution was always bigger than the individual and sometimes crushed him or her with its burdens and traditions.

Now the special moments and creative missions you share with your partner will fit you both perfectly,

And can last far longer, with more fulfillment and richness, than the institutions of old.

How Many Moments Are There in a Second?

· Describe your fantasy of a perfect day with your loved one:

—What are you feeling when you wake up?

_____

_____

—How do you spend the morning, afternoon, and evening? Where?

_____

_____

_____

—How are you relating to the person you're with? What does it feel like?

_____

_____

—What do you talk about?

_____

_____

—How comfortable do you feel during the silences?

_____

—What do you eat?

_____

—What do you wear?

_____

—What is your loved one wearing?

_____

—What's the weather like?

_____

—What do you ask your loved one that you've never asked
anyone before?

_____

_____

—What do you feel about your loved one on that day?

_____

—What do you feel about yourself on that day?

_____

—What other details or feelings can you add?

_____

_____

_____

· Could you create a thousand different "perfect days" with
a partner using these same guidelines?   —Yes   —No
If not, why not? _____

DAY

Whether you call it fertilizer or
something else—it sure makes
things grow.

—ANONYMOUS

What Do You Do with a Problem?

No matter how much you improve yourself,
Love yourself,
Open yourself up to others,
And enjoy your experience,
There's a tiny voice in the back of your head
That whispers, "Don't be foolish—it won't work."

You're terrified there's a problem you haven't solved,
A block you haven't removed,
Or a resistance that won't go away.
And you think that problems are what stand between you
and what you want in life.

It would be great if life worked that way—
Solve your problems and then glide down easy street.
But it doesn't and it never will.

Problems are the food you eat for breakfast.
If you're creative, they turn into nourishment.
If you're not, indigestion.

No matter how wonderful you and your partner are,
Your relationship is still going to have problems.

Yet problems are not what stand between you and what you
want in life.
Running from problems can be your downfall.
Dwelling on problems can be your constant burden.

Never putting your problems to good use can block you from having what you want.
But problems, in themselves, cannot.

Instead of fearing the problems and crises in your relationship, view them as teachers.
They tell you and your partner what areas need attention.
They make you look at who you are, what you want, and how to grow, again and again and again.
They'll show you that you're never finished building a love that lasts.
And though you may not like them at first, you know they're really fertilizer in disguise.

What Do You Do with a Problem?

Today's exercise is the blueprint for turning every problem in your relationship into an opportunity for personal growth. You may have to dig deeply for the honest answers, but the benefits are enormous.

· What obstacle stands between you and happiness in a relationship?

_____

· How long have you had that obstacle?

_____

· What personal benefit do you get (indirectly or secretly— no matter how strange it may seem) from *keeping* that obstacle?

_____

· What specific things do you do to keep the obstacle in your way?

_____   _____

_____   _____

· What dreaded outcome might happen if the obstacle fell away today?

_____

_____

· Looking back at your answers, do you see how you create the problem?
  __Yes __No

· Do you see how that problem served you at one time?
___Yes ___No

· Are you ready to see what life would be like without the problem?
___Yes ___No

· What steps can you take to turn this problem into a solution?

1. _____
2. _____
3. _____
4. _____
5. _____

DAY *38*

Let there be spaces in your togetherness.

—KAHLIL GIBRAN

Friendship is to feel as one
while remaining two.

—ANNE S.
SWETCHINE

How Do You Keep from Smothering Each Other?

It's possible that you and your partner can become one,
And that one will be *less* than the two of you as individuals.

Or it's possible for one plus one
To sum up to *greater* than two,
But only if you have the freedom to be your own person.

You have your own interests, hobbies, friends, and solitude.
So does your partner.
How to mix the separate times with the together times is an
    art,
With you and your partner as the artists,
And the canvas totally up to you both to give it form.

There's a reliance and a familiarity in a love that lasts
That can free you to feel as one
Even when you're physically apart doing different things.
And a clutching dependence that will make you both feel
    trapped and smothered,
No matter how hard you try to believe you have everything
    in common.

Sometimes you'll feel too close and other times too distant.
But just like an artist using too much red and too many
    swirls,
You'll make your creative decision
And bring the work back into balance,
Without blaming your partner or feeling deprived.

Your love that lasts won't take away the life you love to enjoy.
Nor will it make you into someone you never wanted to be.

With two artists working in tandem,
There will be disagreements and different points of view.
There may even be times when the canvas looks way out of
balance.
But you'll always have more paint, more canvas, and more
time to make it right,
Not by compromising toward mediocrity,
But by coming up with good ideas, personal preferences, and
loving solutions that enrich you both.

How Do You Keep from Smothering Each Other?

· Make a list of ten hobbies, interests, and friends you'd like
  to enjoy on your own, without necessarily including your
  partner.

  _____   _____
  _____   _____
  _____   _____
  _____   _____
  _____   _____

· Are you willing to share your insights, excitement, and
  growth from these experiences with your partner?
  __Yes __No If no, why not? _____
  _____

· Are you willing to give your partner the freedom to pursue
  his or her ten solo interests without you?
  __Yes __No If no, why not? _____
  _____

DAY *39*

In the unconscious, every one of us is
convinced of our immortality.

—SIGMUND FREUD

How Much Time Do You Have to Get It Right?

Some people give themselves a week
To attain their dreams,
And then get frustrated when it takes longer.

You'll need some time to build a love that lasts.
Not just to find and open up to the right partner.
But time to let the foundation set,
And for the structure to be built without haste,
And for changes to be planned, discussed, and put into action.

You'll need patience to persist through the ups and downs,
And an open mind to look for the lessons behind every crisis.

If you're ready to give up at the drop of a hat,
The hat will surely fall.
And you'll be pleasantly dissatisfied as you say, "I told you so."

If you're in the habit of testing people
And finding fault as quickly as possible,
You'll have a field day on any human.
And be able to say with defiant joy, "There's no one quite
    right for me."

Forty days is a short time to learn all that it takes.
Yet it's long enough to give you the framework on which to
    base your creative work,
As you build a love that lasts.

Setting deadlines will only make your creative process a
   miserable one.
You're allowed to make mistakes and start over again.
You're allowed to take a rest and give yourself some breathing space.

No matter how young or old you think you are,
There's more than enough time.
Don't be stingy with your horizons,
And don't jump ship every time there's a storm.

How Much Time Do You Have to Get It Right?

· Just for the fun of it, try to answer the following questions:

—How long did it take Noah to build his ark?

———————————

—How long did it take to build the Pyramids?

———————————

—How many days did it take to build Rome?

———————————

—How long did it take Michelangelo to paint the Sistine Chapel?

———————————

—How many years of research went into landing the first man on the moon?

———————————

—How long did it take Francis Ford Coppola to make *Apocalypse Now?*

———————————

—How many months of planning go into the making of a sixty-second advertisement?

———————————

—How much time are you willing to give to building a love that lasts?

———————————

DAY

Happiness is a perfume which you
cannot pour on others without getting
a few drops on yourself.

—LOUIS L. MANN

What's Your Gift?

There's a reason you're here,
And a purpose beyond all the chaos,
A personal meaning beyond all the absurdity.

There's a gift you have
That you can share with the world.

Personal growth is not a one-way street
To the great hot-tub in the sky,
Nor is it something that takes you away from participating
   in the world.

Personal growth is the way to unravel your unique gift,
And to bring it to fruition in the world.

It may be a talent that you possess or a wisdom you can share,
The raising of loving children or service to a worthy enter-
   prise.
It may be one thing or a number of things.
No matter what it is, though, you have it in your possession
And you haven't begun to use it fully.

A love that lasts is the key to opening your heart
To your true essence,
So that you can share it with the world.
It's the channel through which you can stop living inside
   your head,
Always fearful, always alone.

To feel instead the richness of your connection
With those who love and appreciate your unique gift.

You can spend your whole life in protective isolation and
    somber despair,
Never letting anyone see the beauty inside you.
Or you can build the bridge
To do the work that comes from your heart.

For God's sake, you've learned your lessons well.
Now that you're capable of so much more,
Don't pass up the chance.

The gift of love is yours.
Don't keep it to yourself.

What's Your Gift?

· If you knew you had been given a unique talent, what would it be?

_____

· If you knew that you had a mission in life, what would it be?

_____

_____

· If you had a special gift to offer to the world, what would it be?

_____

_____

· How will a love that lasts add to your ability to explore your talent, carry out your mission, and share your gift?

_____

_____

_____

CONCLUSIONS

A colleague of mine told me as I was writing this book, "C'mon, Adelaide, you can't learn everything about a relationship in only forty days. That's ridiculous."
It may seem ridiculous *and* it can be done.

You've completed forty days of lessons and exercises that give you skills and insights toward making the relationship you want come true in your life. And you may be asking yourself the same question—has anything changed for you?

Let's look at what the clues might be. You came into the 40-Day Plan with a certain outlook on relationships. You may have believed they were a burden or a struggle. Or that a good relationship was possible, but not for you.
What's your basic, underlying perception now? Is it more optimistic? More positively realistic? More conscious of the goals and values you have for a relationship? More supported by skills and strengths to overcome your fears and resistances?

What about the skills? Are you going to be able to express your anger without destroying your relationship? Are you going to see the love between you and your partner regardless of all the noise and interference that threaten to make you blind to it? Are you going to be more aware and more honest about your likes and dislikes? More creative in building a relationship that lives up to your goals and capabilities?

I can't tell you how much *you've* learned, but I can tell you that if your basic perspective has shifted, the results can be tremendous. A simple change in how you view yourself, your partner, and your ability to build a love that lasts can make all the difference.

Yet you still might have an underlying fear that something was missing from the 40-Day Plan. There still might be one crisis you don't know how to resolve—one problem area that could still break your heart.

Think back to the forty lessons and exercises you completed. Do you see how many different fears, beliefs, and attitudes you uncovered? Do you see how many preferences, goals, and pleasures you revealed? Do you see how many specific skills and problem-solving techniques you acquired?

There may be situations and conflicts that were not specifically mentioned in the forty days. Yet the lessons and exercises can handle them as well. The forty days include the basic information and steps you need to take no matter what the problem. When a new situation arises, don't panic. Just assume the forty days will work for you. Think back on some of the exercises and techniques. Then find the one that will work for that new situation. The answer will be there for you.

To help you in using the 40-Day Plan as an ongoing support for your relationship, the Conclusions section includes a list of some of the most pressing conflict areas and the lessons and exercises in the 40-Day Plan that deal directly with those areas. When you're having a conflict over sex, money, anger, fear, jealousy, depression, or surviving the big fight, look at the list of sections that deal with that problem and then begin to review the days that covered them.

This book should continue to support you no matter how many times you read it or review it. In fact, the more worn the pages, the more you'll gain from the Plan. Put the book in a special place on your coffee table or next to your bed. And don't let a crisis happen in your relationship without using the techniques in the Plan or referring back to the actual descriptions in the Plan.

A new relationship or a changing relationship can be a shaky and scary time. But if you share the lessons and exercises in this book with your partner, you can begin to find out how to work together toward a successful relationship. The 40-Day Plan is an enjoyable way for the two of you to find a common element between you, a common structure in the goals and values you hold in your relationship.

You might not want to hand out the book on a first date, but after a while you need to know whether your partner is willing to go the relationship road with you. And this is an easy way to see how committed the two of you are to having your relationship work.

Finally, you will want to see how you have put the 40-Day Plan into practice in your relationship. How much are you using the skills? Which ones are you still avoiding?

By completing the 40-Day Plan, you are now a pioneer in the field of men and women who want a new way of relating to each other. These are people who still value the intimate relationship and the strength of a loving commitment. Yet they are also explorers and experimenters who will not settle for the limitations and setbacks that have plagued relationships in the past.

I want you to see yourself as a special person willing to risk truth and honesty in a way that relationships never have before.

I want you to give yourself credit for asking for a great deal —and having the good sense to know you will need skills, persistence, and time to make it happen in your life.

I'd love to hear from you. And most of all, I wish you the best as you continue to find and build a love that lasts.

Congratulations! You've completed the 40-Day Plan.

WHERE TO REVIEW SPECIFIC TOPICS
IN THE 40-DAY PLAN

Crisis Topic	Days
Sex	*13, 15, 19, 21, 22, 25, 31, 34, 36*
Money	*5, 6, 13, 15, 18, 19, 24, 34, 37, 40*
Anger	*7, 10, 11, 23, 26, 27, 29, 35, 37*
Fear	*2, 3, 4, 5, 8, 16, 35, 37, 39*
Jealousy	*1, 7, 10, 20, 23, 26, 27*
Depression	*3, 4, 5, 8, 12, 21, 28, 37, 40*
Surviving the Big Fight	*3, 4, 10, 11, 26, 27, 29, 30, 32, 35, 37*